Examining Government Surveillance Programs and the Conflict of Individual Privacy with National Security Interests.

Comparative Study between Great Britain and the United States of America

Mohamed Rashid Al Balushi

ISBN-13: 978-1979270359

ISBN-10: 197927035X

Mohamed Rashid Al Balushi

CONTENTS

1. Government Surveillance Programs in the United States of America.......................................**14**

      FBI, NSA & CIA

   i. Executive Order 12333

   ii. USA PATRIOT Act of 2001. Section 215

   iii. Foreign Intelligence Surveillance Act of 1978. Section 702

   iv. Transparency of Government Surveillance Programs and the FISC

2. Government Surveillance Programs in Great Britain..**88**

      MI5, MI6, & GCHQ

   i. Regulation of Investigatory Powers Act of 2000

   ii. Telecommunication Act of 1984

   iii. Protection of Freedoms Act of 2012

   iv. Investigatory Powers Act of 2016

TABLE OF DOCUMENTS

TABLE OF ABBREVIATIONS

Central Intelligence Agency (CIA)

Federal Bureau of Investigations (FBI)

Foreign Intelligence Surveillance Act (FISA)

Foreign Intelligence Surveillance Court (FISC)

General Communications Headquarters (GCHQ)

General Data Protection Regulation (GDPR)

National Security Agency (NSA)

Secret Intelligence Services (MI6)

Security Service (MI5)

Signal Intelligence (SIGINT)

"If men were angels, no government would be necessary. If angels were to govern men, neither external nor internal controls on government would be necessary. In framing a government which is to be administered by men over men, the great difficulty lies in this: You must first enable the government to control the governed; and in the next place, oblige it to control itself."[1]

James Madison

Author of The Federalist No. 51

James Madison, the author of Federalist No. 51 and a founding father who served as the fourth President of the United States, addressed and advocated the necessity of creating checks and balances in government, in addition to the clear separation of powers within the government. Although Madison and the founding fathers could not have foreseen the evolution of technology and the challenges this would create for the privacy protections and constitutional rights that were ratified 238 years ago, it is vital that we consider the warning Madison has given in the above statement. The United States government surveillance programs have been a topic of heated

---

[1] James Madison, The Structure of the Government Must Furnish the Proper Checks and Balances Between the Different Departments, The Federalist No. 51 (Feb 6, 1788), http://www.constitution.org/fed/federa51.htm

debate since September 11, 2001, and the fumes have been further ignited after the Snowden revelations in 2013.

Those government surveillance programs have created some sort of disparity within the American community, with the government on one side advocating for such programs on the basis that it combats terrorism, and opponents arguing that the privacy of the American people has been compromised due to the mass collection of data from communications and the internet. Such surveillance programs may be perceived by some as an infrastructure of tyranny - relating to Madison's warning relating to governmental tyranny - yet, they may also be portrayed as a protection of national security at any cost. In relation to the checks and balances, the Foreign Intelligence Surveillance Court[2] was established to oversee requests for surveillance warrants and it has even been perceived as a court almost parallel to the United States Supreme Court. However, such a court has been subject to scrutiny in multiple occasions die to its lack of transparency, appointment process, and allegations of bias.

---

[2] http://www.fisc.uscourts.gov/ "The Foreign Intelligence Surveillance Court was established by Congress in 1978. The Court entertains applications made by the United States Government for approval of electronic surveillance, physical search, and certain other forms of investigative actions for foreign intelligence purposes."

While my position on governmental surveillance programs has not yet been established, I have a strong belief that such surveillance is necessary for the protection of national security, which in turn serves an important role in protecting and shielding both individuals and the government from terrorism. Nevertheless, as a proponent of safeguarding privacy, this book aims to address the concerns and issues that are present in government surveillance programs and that although such programs do provide some sort of privacy protections, they do not provide the necessary and adequate privacy protections individuals desire.

Even prior to recent events, such as the NSA halting its 'about' searches under the upstream program and the USA Freedom Act amendments to both the Foreign Intelligence Surveillance Act and the USA PATRIOT Act [3] - which are to be discussed in further sections - the 2013 Snowden leaks are what initially sparked this topic in both local and global media. In June 2013, Edward Snowden, a former contractor for the Central Intelligence Agency (CIA), leaked top-secret documents to the media regarding internet and phone

---

[3] Uniting and Strengthening America by Providing Appropriate Tools Required to Intercept and Obstruct Terrorism Act of 2001.

surveillance conducted by the American Intelligence community.[4]

Journalists have released more than 7000 top-secret documents entrusted to them by Edward Snowden.[5] The documents outline the National Security Agency hacking military computer systems in China and in Hong Kong,[6] and the taping of fibre-optic cables by the British Government Communications Headquarters to collect and store global email messages, calls, and Facebook posts, and share such information with the National Security Agency.[7] The leaks also contained various documents demonstrating the cooperation between Britain and the United States in monitoring social media and the NSA permitting the GCHQ to access its data without supervision.[8]

As the leaks brought American-British intelligence activities to light, they have sparked major controversy both within the American and British communities – and perhaps even the international community. In quoting Sir David Omand, Former

---

[4] Edward Snowden: Leaks that exposed US spy programme, BBC: News (Jan 17, 2014), http://www.bbc.com/news/world-us-canada-23123964

[5] Paul Szoldra, This is everything Edward Snowden revealed in one year of unprecedented top-secret leaks, Business Insider (Sep 16, 2016), http://www.businessinsider.com/snowden-leaks-timeline-2016-9

[6] Revealed on June 13, 2013.

[7] Revealed on June 21, 2013.

[8] Revealed on April 30, 2014.

No. 10 adviser, in his response to the GCHQ being accused of gathering data on online corporations, he labelled the Snowden event as the 'most catastrophic ever,' [9] seeing as such data could have fallen into the hands of enemy States such as Russia and China. Similarly, the United States had an aggressive reaction to the leaks when the Department of Justice charged Edward Snowden with violation of the Espionage Act of 1917 as well as theft of government property.[10] Thus, it can be seen that both intelligence communities viewed the Snowden leaks as irresponsible and damaging to national security of both nations.

Nevertheless, the other side of our debate, which is the privacy of individuals, may have gained momentum as well as some wins. An example may be the European Court of Justice's invalidation of the safe harbour provision in the Schrems case - on October 6, 2015 - between the United States and Europe, which allowed tech corporations, such as Google and Facebook, to transfer personal data relating to European

---

[9] Snowden leaks 'worst ever loss to British intelligence', BBC: News (Oct 11, 2013), http://www.bbc.com/news/uk-24486649

[10] Peter Finn and Sari Horwits, U.S. charges Snowden with espionage, The Washington Post (June 21, 2013), https://www.washingtonpost.com/world/national-security/us-charges-snowden-with-espionage/2013/06/21/507497d8-dab1-11e2-a016-92547bf094cc_story.html?utm_term=.858fa777d372

individuals to servers in the United States. In this case, the court made it clear that due to the unfettered access of American intelligence agencies to data, they were thus also infringing on Europeans' right to privacy.[11] On July 12, 2016, the European Commission adopted the EU - US privacy shield that places stronger privacy requirements on American corporations when transferring personal data from the European Union to the United States. Another example may be the United States Senate passage of the USA Freedom Act on June 2, 2015. The Act modified several provisions of the USA PATRIOT Act and the Foreign Intelligence Surveillance Act. Although this Act restored several surveillance sections in both the PATRIOT Act and FISA, it also limited the government's bulk data collection - the USA Freedom Act amendments are a critical part of this book. This demonstrates that there is a shift towards protecting privacy rights, to at least a greater extent than that prior to the Snowden leaks.

Although this book mainly focuses on comparing and examining both governmental surveillance programs in the United States and Great Britain, it is nevertheless vital to demonstrate the cooperation between both nations in conducting surveillance. Hence, this is to be based on the leaks

---

[11] Export.gov. available at: http://2016.export.gov/safeharbor/

provided by Edward Snowden and statements made by those concerned following the leaks. As previously mentioned, the General Communications Headquarters (GCHQ) has been working closely with the NSA under the Tempora program. Tempora is a code name for a secret program used by the GCHQ where the system buffers internet communications after the agency taps fibre-optic cables, hence, such data is retained and shared with the NSA.[12] Moreover, on October 30, 2013, the leaks revealed a joint program between the NSA and the GCHQ called Muscular.[13] By accessing the cables through which the corporations' internal network traffic passes, this program infiltrates and copies data flowing out of Google's and Yahoo's data centres.[14] Ultimately, this all reflects that both intelligence communities have been taking advantage of the vast amount of data stored in and transferred between global data centres.

---

[12] As revealed by Snowden on June 21, 2013.

[13] Barton Gellman and Ashkan Soltani, NSA infiltrates links to Yahoo, Google data centres worldwide, Snowden documents say, The Washington Post (Oct 30, 2013), https://www.washingtonpost.com/world/national-security/nsa-infiltrates-links-to-yahoo-google-data-centers-worldwide-snowden-documents-say/2013/10/30/e51d661e-4166-11e3-8b74-d89d714ca4dd_story.html?utm_term=.d81aca03ddd7

[14] Grace Eden, Muscular, Digital Citizenship and Surveillance Society (July 22, 2015), http://www.dcssproject.net/muscular/

The recent Manchester terror attacks in the United Kingdom that involved a suicide bombing carried out during an Ariana Grande concert [15] reflected the close relationship between both the American and British intelligence community. Following the attacks, and as the name of the perpetrators was given to the United States intelligence community under confidentiality, the information was leaked to the American media, which lead to fury and condemnation from the British Home Secretary Amber Rudd.[16] As a result of the leak, Greater Manchester Police stopped sharing information with the U.S. due to outrage from UK officials and the failure of U.S. intelligence agencies to protect secure information.[17] Nevertheless, it has been reported by several news agencies, such as CNN and Sky, that after a brief meeting between Trump and May, intelligence sharing between both nations resumed as Trump vowed to investigate the leaks and described them as 'deeply troubling.'[18]

---

[15] The Attack occurred at Manchester Arena, England, on May 22, 2017. Claire Phipps, Haroon Siddique, Matthew Weaver and Kevin Rawlinson, UK agrees to resume sharing intelligence with US after assurances – as it happened, The Guardian (May 26, 2017), https://www.theguardian.com/uk-news/live/2017/may/25/manchester-attack-police-raids-terror-network-live-updates

[16] Manchester Attack: US leaks about bomber irritating - Rudd, BBC News: UK Politics (May 24, 2017), http://www.bbc.com/news/election-2017-40026413

[17] Manchester attack: Police not sharing information with US, BBC News (May 25, 2017), http://www.bbc.com/news/uk-politics-40040210

[18] Kevin Liptak and Jeff Zeleny, US - UK intel sharing back on after Trump vows to plug leaks, CNN Politics (May 25, 2017), http://www.cnn.com/2017/05/25/politics/nato-trump-intel-sharing/index.html

The Manchester attacks leak was detrimental to the entire investigation, as the names of suspects should have been kept confidential which may therefore reflect a possible lack of confidentiality within the White House under the Trump administration. Thus, the suspension of intelligence sharing by Britain could send a message to the U.S. reflecting anger and the necessity to protect sensitive information in order to maintain the integrity of intelligence agencies. Nevertheless, the Manchester incident indicates the strong cooperation between both nations and the speed of actionable intelligence flow between them; all in the name of protecting national security.

The central debate of this book involves the privacy concerns that arise due to government surveillance programs. Generally, and in relation to criticisms related to the United States surveillance programs, the USA PATRIOT Act's passage in October 2001 drew criticisms on Fourth Amendment grounds. Section 215, which is the main focus under this Act, drew criticism on the basis that it permits warrantless searches without the requirement to notify the target. Similarly, with respect to programs such as PRISM and Upstream, the United States government cites Section 702 of the Foreign Intelligence Surveillance Act. Under section 702, the NSA is allowed to collect mass data of phone calls and emails directly from the physical infrastructure of telecommunication providers. Regardless of the resumed statements by directors and those in charge of protecting the fundamental rights of citizens and in increasing transparency of such programs, the arguments continue to ensue in many occasions, for instance, through whistle-blowers such as Snowden.

Nevertheless, this book shall elaborate further on this topic comparing arguments concerning surveillance programs, discussing both defenders of expansive surveillance and defenders of privacy as well as civil liberties. Thus, those that believe that the purpose of such surveillance or intelligence is to protect the nation. In contrast, proponents of privacy tend to focus on the implications of domestic surveillance were such surveillance or mass data collection affects the lives of people in their homes. Yet, proponents of privacy do not call for a complete shutdown of such programs, but for the implementation of stricter safeguards. Generally, both the United States and the British governments advocate for the protection of individual privacy, where the United States places certain safeguards and procedures to protect the privacy of its individuals through legislation, establishing guidelines for conducting intelligence to serve national security. On the other hand, Britain is required under its 1998 Human Rights Act and European laws to protect and safeguard the privacy of individuals, however its recently enacted Investigatory Powers Act challenges such individual protections.

The first section of this book will examine government surveillance programs in the United States of America, both domestic and foreign. We are to look in to the functions and public perceptions of the FBI, NSA, and CIA, and will portray the controversies surrounding their conducts. This section will further look at Executive Order 12333 that has not received as much media attention as other surveillance programs. This will involve examining the history of this Executive Order, its amendments, and the arguments for and against the E.O. An examination of Section 215 of the USA PATRIOT Act and Section 702 of the Foreign Intelligence Surveillance Act will be taken, where we are to look at the history behind both, and the amendments introduced by the USA Freedom Act in 2015. This section will also look into the Foreign Intelligence Surveillance Court and will examine its functions and efficiency in authorizing surveillance programs.

The second section will look at government surveillance programs in Great Britain, domestic, signals and joint intelligence. This section will have a similar flow to the first section where we will examine the functions and public perceptions of MI5, MI6, and the GCHQ, including the controversies surrounding these agencies. A portrayal of government surveillance and its development under case law within Britain will also be presented. This section will ultimately look at the regulations governing government surveillance in Great Britain, those include; Regulation of Investigatory Powers Act 2000, which is the main piece of legislation as it grants and regulates the powers of public bodies to carry out surveillance and investigation. The Telecommunication Act 1984 that concerns the facilitating of bulk communications data collection. The Protection of Freedoms Act 2012 that concerns the controlling or the restricting of collection, storage, retention, and use of information in Governmental databases. Finally, the Investigatory Powers Act of 2016, which performs, targeted interception of communications, the bulk collection of communications data, and the bulk interception of communications. Thereafter, the effectiveness and criticisms of such statutes will be examined.

The third section of the book will look at the tensions between privacy and security under the surveillance programs, also known as the privacy dilemma. This section will examine both the United States and Britain's stance on privacy and how they honour such protections embedded in their laws. With regards to the United States, we will look at how the programs treat individuals, and the stance of the Fourth Amendment to the United States Constitution when it comes to surveillance programs. In relation to the United Kingdom, we will also look at how the programs affect individuals and how the Human Rights Act of 1998 acts for the protection of the privacy of individuals and other rights. The fourth section will present a general comparative study of the surveillance programs in both the States and Britain which will be based on the previous three sections. The fifth and final section of this book will be entitled 'Recommendations,' where we are to highlight the necessity of undertaking "privacy by design" approach when developing surveillance tools.

This book will look at surveillance, privacy and related laws as it aims to suggest the necessity of accomplishing both end goals, which are the protection of national security and the protection of individual rights, specifically privacy. Furthermore, we are to examine how intelligence has brought forward a troubled and evolving relationship between both foreign and domestic surveillance in recent years. Ultimately, we aim to conclude that foreign intelligence gathering is vital to the protection of national security but that individuals have the right to enjoy stronger privacy protections, thus, governments must maintain a balance. Nevertheless, it ought to be stated that as we are in the twenty first century and governments seek to be protected from international terrorism and regulate daily life, clandestine intelligence will be conducted on a considerable scale. Hence, conducting intelligence gathering and protecting the privacy of individuals are two notions that may be seen to be in conflict with each other unless significant steps are taken by governments, such as the recommendation of a privacy by design approach when drafting or reauthorizing laws.

1. Government Surveillance Programs in the United States of America

The Federal Bureau of Investigation (FBI), The National Security Agency (NSA), and The Central Intelligence Agency (CIA) are all integral parts of the United States intelligence community. Although the United States Intelligence Community (IC) is a federation of 16 separate agencies, these three have been mentioned due to their direct association and control over the governmental surveillance programs that we are to discuss, section 215 of the USA PATRIOT Act and section 702 of the Foreign Intelligence Act. These three agencies are the most important and sophisticated in the American intelligence community, although they have separate responsibilities, they share the mission of protecting the United States from both domestic and foreign harm and threats. The aforementioned three agencies are not only concerned with security and intelligence, but also with law enforcement. Indeed, much of what they perform is integral to both domestic and international security.

The FBI is a domestic law enforcement agency that gathers domestic intelligence and combats threats emanating from within the United States. Thus, in the event that an individual within the United States was planning to do something that would threaten the safety and security of the nation, then the investigation would be under the FBI's jurisdiction. In addition, as the FBI handles domestic surveillance, if the NSA or CIA requested information on American individuals then they must go through the FBI in order to obtain such information.

The NSA deals with foreign intelligence gathering where it is responsible for global monitoring, collection, and processing of information for counterintelligence and national security purposes. Generally, the NSA is a cryptological organization as it decrypts foreign intelligence and creates encryption codes to protect the security of American persons. Thus, it performs both code-breaking and code-making as it is tasked with protecting the United States communication networks and systems. These are known as signals intelligence activities (SIGINT).

In addition, the NSA's Information Assurance (IA) mission - executed by the NSA's Information Assurance Directorate (IAD) - serves a unique role in laying down a set of measures intended to protect information and information systems that handle classified information, which are also critical to intelligence activities.[19] Although the IA's mission is mainly defensive - protecting the nation's systems - the NSA also has an offensive mission in which it carries out signal intelligence. So while the IAD seeks to patch security holes in the nation's internet infrastructure, the NSA's signals intelligence directorate seek to find such holes and keep them open to spy

---

[19] NSA CSS, Information Assurance. Available at: https://www.nsa.gov/what-we-do/information-assurance/

on foreign adversaries. Thus, there appears to be conflict between both activities, and even if both directorate's fully merged, the signals intelligence mission will absorb the IA mission as it is bigger in size and more dominating. Indeed, the NSA's work and mission mainly involves conducting foreign intelligence or counterintelligence, but the agency has also been able to conduct domestic surveillance alongside the FBI, which has caused concern in the privacy arena as well as facing litigation due to its violation of the constitutional rights of American persons.

Finally, the CIA gathers, processes, and analyses information internationally as long as it is relevant to the security of the United States. The CIA, unlike the NSA, gathers its information and data via human intelligence and not through signals intelligence activities. Hence, the CIA has agents all over the world reporting back to the central offices in Washington. In addition, the CIA's roles include covert paramilitary operations, conducting and overseeing covert action at the behest of the President of the United States, and counterterrorism as the top priority besides counterintelligence. Thus, the main difference between the CIA and the NSA is that the CIA gathers and analyses information on foreign governments and individuals, while the NSA gathers and analyses foreign communications.

Those agencies are worth mentioning briefly in the outset of this chapter due to the fact that each one is concerned with a different area of focus, yet, as will be discussed, they do occasionally cooperate on cases involving terrorism or espionage by sharing information which could thus lead to breakthroughs. Ultimately, the United States intelligence agencies all share a common mission, which is to protect the United States from threats whilst preserving the privacy of American individuals.

In the United States of America, there are three main legal regimes for the surveillance of networks, these are, Executive Order 12333, section 215 of the USA PATRIOT Act, and notably section 702 of the Foreign Intelligence Surveillance Act.

i.   Executive Order 12333

Executive Order 12333 may have received little media attention, specifically after the Snowden revelations, where much of the attention was paid to both section 215 and section

702. Nevertheless, E.O. 12333 can be portrayed as serving as an alternate basis of authority for surveillance activities, above section 215 and section 702. As an overview E.O. 12333 was signed on December 4, 1981, by then U.S. President Ronald Reagan. The E.O. was regarded by the American intelligence community as a vital document providing authority for the expansion of data collection activities, where only data existing outside the United States is covered under E.O. 12333. The NSA considers the E.O. it to be the primary legal authority for the collection of data flowing through the data centres of communication giants such as Google and Yahoo.[20] Additionally, unlike other NSA programs such as PRISM and Upstream, which we are to elaborate on further on in this section, the NSA has unlimited authority under E.O. 12333 as it can access a trove of information and tap phones and internet backbones throughout the world, but not in the United States.

In addition, E.O. 12333 has been amended three times; it was amended by E.O. 13284 on January 23, 2003, by E.O. 13555 on August 27, 2004, and by EO 13470 on July 30· 2008.[21] Regardless of the broad authority E.O. 12333 established for

---

[20] Francesca Bignami, European versus American liberty: A comparative privacy analysis of antiterrorism data mining, 48 Boston College Law Review. 609 (2007).
[21] Executive Order 12333. Available at: https://fas.org/irp/offdocs/eo/eo-12333-2008.pdf

the intelligence community, the aforementioned amendments were mainly administrative. For instance, E.O. 13555 and E.O. 13470, mainly supplemented and strengthened the role of the Director of National Intelligence, thus, suppressing the authority the CIA previously had as the head of the intelligence community.

In examining E.O. 12333, or Executive Orders in general, the following points are to portray the arguments for and the criticisms that E.O. 12333 may be subjected to, or is already subjected to by various personnel. There is no doubt that the text of the Executive Order 12333, even after the amendments, has an overall goal, which is to ensure the President - regardless of the political party - as well as the senior officials in the Security Council, have the necessary information to deliver decisions that protect the United States from foreign threats. Nevertheless, U.S. persons are not an exception to having their information collected, retained, or disseminated by the intelligence community,[22] which thus raises concerns.

Executive Order 12333 may actually be described as a loophole to the privacy of individuals. John Napier Tye, a

---

[22] E.O. 12333. Part 2. 2.3

former Obama State Department official, wrote on Op-Ed in the Washington Post that "I believe that Americans should be even more concerned about the collection and storage of their communications under Executive Order 12333 than under section 215 of the USA PATRIOT Act.' [23] Under the second section of E.O. 12333, the intelligence community is authorized to collect mass data of American individuals abroad, when they speak to others abroad, or when their calls are deliberately diverted abroad. In addition, the collection of data belonging to Americans is permitted under ten circumstances under 2.3 of E.O. 12333, including the unintentional collection of data of a U.S. person, and where such data can be retained. This section does not even require that the U.S. person has committed a wrongdoing, thus, it may be perceived that no limits are required for the volume of communications that can be collected and thus retained. Indeed, minimization procedures relating to data of American individuals are outlined under the second section of E.0. 12333, but they are subjected to criticism as it will be portrayed in the upcoming paragraph. Another example may be that the text of E.O. 12333 contains no

---

[23] John Napier Tye, Meet Executive Order 12333: The Reagan rule that lets the NSA spy on Americans, The Washington Post (July 18, 2014), https://www.washingtonpost.com/opinions/meet-executive-order-12333-the-reagan-rule-that-lets-the-nsa-spy-on-americans/2014/07/18/93d2ac22-0b93-11e4-b8e5-d0de80767fc2_story.html?utm_term=.6c415befaca6

provision that prevents the NSA from collecting all sorts of communications, for instance the sole collection of metadata, thus, without a warrant or even a court approval. The NSA can sweep as much data as it wants as long as it is conducted outside the United States in the course of a foreign intelligence investigation.

This second section of E.O. 12333 covers what information can be collected, how such information is to be collected, and what can be shared about U.S. persons. The current guidelines, the USSID 18, [24] or the United States Signals Intelligence Directive SP0018, provide implementation guidance and direction to NSA employees, ensuring that laws, executive orders, and constitutional principles are implemented within the United States Signal Intelligence. Although the USSID 18 can be perceived as outlining minimization procedures in collecting, retaining, and sharing information relating to U.S. persons, its rules and exceptions are very narrow and vague. For instance, or even probably the main problem, under Section 4, the definition of 'intentional targeting of U.S. persons' is very narrow. Also, although a warrant is required from the FISA Court to intercept communications of American persons, the

---

[24] USSID 18. Available at;
https://www.dni.gov/files/documents/1118/CLEANEDFinal USSID SP0018.pdf

exceptions overruling the warrant requirement go on for four pages.[25] Thus, the minimization procedures can be seen as a substantial loophole, especially because such a directive allows for the extensive use of personal information relating to Americans without a probable cause warrant due to the heavily redacted exceptions.

Just recently, prior to his departure from office, President Obama, on January 12, 2017, put into place amendments to E.O. 12333 on the NSA's sharing of raw signals intelligence information with the rest of the intelligence community.[26] It is therefore obvious that the personal data of many American individuals would circle around the intelligence community in bulk, which may thus give rise to privacy concerns. Prior to the administration's decision, the NSA was tasked with collecting, handling, and filtering the surveillance information for the rest of the government, passing on only what deemed relevant to other agencies. The NSA also masked names and other information related to individuals that were not relevant to an investigation, thus, minimization procedures were implemented. It can therefore be concluded that the NSA will

---

[25] Ibid.

[26] Jane Chong, Obama administration releases long awaited new E.O. 12333 rules on sharing of raw signals intelligence information within IC, LAWFARE: Surveillance (2017)

share such raw materials with other agencies without implementing the necessary privacy protections, such as disseminating the data and masking the identity and communications of callers.

Therefore, this decision by the administration is an irritation to privacy advocates, where the collection of the bulk data under E.O. 12333 is already conducted without requiring a warrant. Nevertheless, Susan Hennessey, the managing editor of Lawfare, has stated in an interview that those final changes by Obama prior to leaving office can be attributed to the fact that the Obama administration wanted to make it harder for President Trump to encroach even further on privacy and civil liberties.[27] Nevertheless, it can be said that it was an oversight on the Obama administration's part in not appointing an independent oversight board for E.O. 12333, similar to the Privacy and Civil Liberties Oversight Board (PCLOB) - a bipartisan agency within the Executive Branch created by Congress to advise the President and senior officials to ensure that concerns related to privacy and civil liberties are taken into

---

[27] Kaveh Waddell, Why Is Obama Expanding Surveillance Powers Right before He Leaves Office? It could be to prevent Trump from extending them even more., The Atlantic (Jan 13, 2017), https://www.theatlantic.com/technology/archive/2017/01/obama-expanding-nsa-powers/513041/

consideration in the development of laws - that provides key insight into the section 215 and section 702 programs. Ultimately, and in quoting Senator Dianne Feinstein (D-CA), where she stated that 'I do not think privacy protections are built into it [E.O. 12333].'[28] Thus, seeing as the collection of data is large on the front end, there should be a requirement of tightening the minimization procedures on the back end.

In relation to the lack of oversight, it ought to be stated that it is unacceptable that governmental agencies, especially intelligence agencies that generally have broad authority, exercise said authority without any oversight, neither by the U.S. Congress nor by the Judiciary. This is also the case with E.O. 12333. As with all executive orders, E.O. 12333 is purely under the Executive's Branch's control, thus Congress and the Judiciary both have authority to a certain extent or even interests in the operations of such orders as there are few legislative reviews and a lack of court reviews regarding the surveillance operations. In addition, executive orders have been vested in Presidents under Article II of the U.S. Constitution where the President is made the commander in chief and are required to take care that the laws be faithfully executed.[29]

---

[28] Executive Order 12333, epic.org, https://epic.org/privacy/surveillance/12333/
[29] U.S. Const. art II

Generally, executive orders can only direct federal agencies on the implementation of laws, which thus grants Congress to pass a law to override the executive order as long as a presidential veto is awarded. This is challenging to obtain, as it is dependent upon the current commander in chief's position in relation to their predecessor. Therefore, although the amendments that have been introduced to E.O. 12333 throughout the years - E.O. 13284 on January 23, 2003, E.O. 13555 on August 27, 2004, and EO 13470 on July 30, 2008 - provide that there should be a requirement of compliance with congressional oversight,[30] E.O. 12333 was originally instated without any congressional or judicial oversight. Thus, in quoting Senator Dianne Feinstein (D-CA), 'The executive controls intelligence in the country.'[31]

However, with a proper oversight board of E.O. 12333, and by ensuring that the actions taken by the executive branch in protecting national security are balanced with the need to protect the privacy and civil liberties of Americans, PCLOB could have a greater role in overseeing the E.O. and reviewing its implementation. Most importantly, PCLOB should be given full access to all information categorized as classified by the IC

---

[30] Executive Order 12333. United States Intelligence Activities. Part 3. Section 301. Congressional Oversight.

[31] Executive Order 12333, epic.org, https://epic.org/privacy/surveillance/12333/

in order to ease its performance in protecting privacy and civil liberties.[32] PCLOB should not only take into consideration the issue of privacy and what type of data is accessed, but also the entire scope of information under E.O. 12333 and to stress the requirement for greater oversight, by Congress, the judiciary, and the public. Ultimately, although PCLOB did publicly state in 2015 that it intends to review the counterterrorism activities conducted by the Intelligence Community under E.O. 12333,[33] and not only base their attention on section 215 of the USA PATRIOT Act and section 702 of FISA, but the Board is currently without an Executive Director and has only one standing serving member (Elisebeth C Cook).[34] Thus, PCLOB would have not been capable of performing a proper review and critical oversight of E.O. 12333 as it lacks the element of having qualified members to make sure that intelligence programs safeguard the privacy and civil liberties of individuals.

ii.   The USA PATRIOT Act of 2001. Section 215

---

[32] Overview of PCLOB's role and functions. Available at: https://www.pclob.gov/
[33] PCLOB, April 8, 2015 Public Meeting. Available at:
https://www.pclob.gov/events/2015/april08.html
[34] David Hoffman and Riccardo Masucci, Swift PCLOB appointments for a more robust Privacy Shield, NEWEUROPE (July 3, 2017),
https://www.neweurope.eu/article/swift-pclob-appointments-robust-privacy-shield/

The second legal regime that we are to look at is section 215 of the USA PATRIOT Act [35] that was signed into law in October 26, 2001, by President George W. Bush. Congress passed the USA PATRIOT Act in response to the September 11, 2001, terrorist attacks, whereby the search and surveillance powers of the intelligence community and federal law enforcement were expanded, thus, the legislation was pushed to strengthen security controls. Section 215 of the USA PATRIOT Act amended Title V, Section 501, of the Foreign Intelligence Surveillance Act 1978, which is concerned with 'access to certain business records for foreign intelligence and international terrorism investigations.'[36]

American Civil Liberties Union v. James Clapper [37] is a landmark federal case worth mentioning as the lawsuit came in the wake of disclosures by Edward Snowden about the NSA surveillance programs. On June 11, 2013, the ACLU filed a lawsuit challenging the legality of the NSA's mass data collection of American's phone records where the ACLU

---

[35] Full title: Uniting and Strengthening America by Providing Appropriate Tools Required to Intercept and Obstruct Terrorism Act of 2001.
[36] 50 U.S.C. sec. 1861
[37] American Civil Liberties Union v. James Clapper, 959 F.Supp.2d 724 (S.D.N.Y. 2013)

argued - as Verizon subscribers - that the bulk collection violates their freedoms of speech and association protected by the First Amendment, in addition to their right to privacy protected by the Fourth Amendment. The case was triggered when the Guardian reported, on June 5, 2013, that the FISC, after a request submitted by the NSA, ordered Verizon, an American telecom provider, to hand over communication records of millions of U.S. customers.[38] Thus, the Snowden revelation reflected the indiscriminate bulk collection of data, regardless of whether the person is suspected of any wrongdoing, of millions of American individuals. The court ruled that the bulk collection of data was constitutional as it did not violate the Fourth Amendment. Nevertheless, the ACLU appealed and on May 7, 2015, the United States Court of Appeals for the Second Circuit ruled that bulk collection of data was not authorized under Section 215 of the USA Patriot Act.[39] In summary, the judges in the latter case ruled that the law does not authorize the government to collect data in bulk, thus, if Section 215 was to be authorized by June 2, 2015 - as will be discussed below - then the government will have to

---

[38] Glenn Greenwald, NSA collecting phone records of millions of Verizon customers daily, The Guardian (June 6, 2013), https://www.theguardian.com/world/2013/jun/06/nsa-phone-records-verizon-court-order

[39] American Civil Liberties Union v. James Clapper, 785 F.3d 787 (2ND Cir., 2015)

discontinue its bulk collection of data under the program, unless Congress provides otherwise in writing.

Section 215 of the USA PARTIOT Act was reauthorized numerously as well as amended throughout the years.[40] Nevertheless, on June 1, 2015, and following a lack of congressional approval, certain provisions of the USA PATRIOT Act expired. Yet, on June 2, 2015, The USA Freedom Act [41] was enacted in order to restore in a modified form certain provisions of the USA PATRIOT Act. Section 215 of the USA Patriot Act, which concerns the collection of foreign intelligence data that does not concern U.S. persons, and if the data sought is related to a U.S. person then it must be relevant to the prevention of terrorism or espionage, and not solely based on activities protected by the First Amendment. However, the National Security Agency has been secretly collecting the phone records of millions of Americans from numerous telephone communication providers through a series of renewed requests by the FBI. As the storage of such bulk metadata presents a risk to the personal privacy and civil liberty

---

[40] "As of July 31, 2013, the FISC had reauthorized the program 34 times under 14 different judges." Available at: https://www.csis.org/analysis/fact-sheet-section-215-usa-patriot-act

[41] Full title: Uniting and Strengthening America by Fulfilling Rights and Ending Eavesdropping, Dragnet-collection and Online Monitoring Act.

of Americans, the USA Freedom Act amended section 215 of the USA PATRIOT Act whereby the data is to be held by private telecommunication providers, and the NSA can only obtain data about targeted individuals after obtaining permission from the FISC.[42] Generally, the USA Freedom Act imposes limits on the FBI's and NSA's bulk collection of metadata from telecommunications providers on United States citizens. Section 215 was thus extended through 2019 and the NSA will be working with providers, rather than requesting bulk data. Hence, section 215 provides legal basis for obtaining calling records in the form of metadata, where only the technical details of a conversation are shown, not the content of any telephone conversation.

To elaborate further on the functions of Section 215, it would be adequate to state that following the Snowden leaks, as earlier portrayed, the American society was made more aware of the probably slightly concealed surveillance programs, such as the section 215 program that was hastily adopted following September 11, 2001, attacks. Section 215 is also known as the library records - business records or tangible things provision -

---

[42] Dan Froomkin, USA Freedom Act: Small step for post-Snowden reform, giant leap for congress, The Intercept_ (June 3, 2015), https://theintercept.com/2015/06/02/one-small-step-toward-post-snowden-surveillance-reform-one-giant-step-congress/

program due to the wide range of personal data investigated. Section 215 amended section 501 of the Foreign Intelligence Surveillance Act as it permits the FBI's collection of "tangible things (including books, records, documents, and other items) (on behalf of NSA) for an investigation to obtain foreign intelligence information." [43] Hence, the collection of the aforementioned items is permitted as long as the investigation is conducted for foreign intelligence purposes that are not concerned with U.S. persons.[44] Yet, in relation to metadata concerning U.S. persons, if the target is a U.S. person, then the investigation must be related to preventing terrorism or espionage, and not solely based on conduct protected by the First Amendment.

As it will be portrayed below, supporters of the USA PATRIOT Act, especially those provisions under Title II, claim that these provisions are necessary for protecting national security and combating terrorism. On the other hand, critics argue that such provisions involving the collection of data infringe upon individual privacy and civil liberties. Although one might perceive that the amendments to section 215 by the

---

[43] Foreign Intelligence Surveillance Act 1978. Section 501. 50 U.S. Code. 1861. a (1)

[44] Foreign Intelligence Surveillance Act 1978. Section 501. 50 U.S. Code. 1861. a (2b)

USA Freedom Act may be considered a victory for privacy rights advocates in Congress, other members of the Senate have opposed the Act, such as Senate Majority Leader Mitch McConnell (R-Ky) who stated that he cannot support the passage of the so-called USA Freedom Act as it does not enhance the privacy protections of individuals and weakens the fighting tools for the government in responding to terrorist threats.[45] Hence, it can be said that there is still great opposition to the idea that existing surveillance programs do not infringe on privacy and that national security should be superior. On the other hand, Senator Mike Lee (R-Utah), stated that the USA Freedom Act protects national security as well as the privacy of Americans. He added that the American people intuitively understand that it is nobody's business to know where their calls are directed.[46]

After outlining the process and functioning of Section 215, it is vital to discuss whether the data collection program under this bill actually promotes the protection of both personal privacy and national security by combating terrorism and espionage. Thus, we now move to the main part of this chapter,

---

[45] Erin Kelly, Senate approves USA Freedom Act, USA TODAY (June 2, 2015), https://www.usatoday.com/story/news/politics/2015/06/02/patriot-act-usa-freedom-act-senate-vote/28345747/
[46] Ibid.

which is analysing the arguments for and against section 215 of the USA PATRIOT Act.

After the horrific attacks of September 11, 2001, the USA PATRIOT Act was signed into law by President George W. Bush on October 26, 2001. Although the idea of intelligence or surveillance has been central to United States state power and to other power nations, the September attacks may have led to the enactment of the USA PATRIOT Act opportunistically as its assertion had been quite vocal. Thus, the Act was hurried through in the name of national security. As the USA PATRIOT ACT was passed by Congress in response to the September 11, 2001, attacks, which occurred domestically, the definition of terrorism has been expanded under the USA PATRIOT Act to cover 'domestic' as opposed to international.[47] As can be deduced from the name, the USA PATRIOT Act is expected to live up to its expectation of providing the appropriate tools required to intercept and obstruct terrorism. The following paragraphs are to present the

---

[47] The USA PATRIOT Act. Section 802. "(5) The term 'domestic terrorism' means activities that -- (A) involve acts dangerous to human life that are a a violation of the criminal laws of the United States or of any State; (B) if the act appears to be intended to: (i) intimidate or coerce a civilian population; (ii) influence the policy of a government by intimidation or coercion; or (iii) to affect the conduct of a government by mass destruction, assassination or kidnapping. (C) Occur primarily within the territorial jurisdiction of the United States" and if they do not, may be regarded as international terrorism.

arguments of how the bill's enactment was to combat terrorism, and not as a surveillance tool which turns regular citizens into suspects.

Following the Second Circuit Court of Appeal ruling, on May 7, 2015, in the American Civil Liberties Union v. Clapper case, where the court declared that the NSA's bulk collection of American phone records was unlawful under Section 215 of the USA PATRIOT Act, several U.S. Senators immediately responded. Four senators, Mitch McConnell, Richard Burr, Tom Cotton, Jeff Sessions, and Marco Rubio, forcefully defended the counterterrorism program 'section 215', as they made some statements that are worth noting in this argument.[48] Although the Senators elaborated on various matters related to the program, specifically the bulk collection of data, we are to solely direct our discussion to that related to terrorism. One of the claims made by McConnell and Rubio in attempting to emphasise the importance of such a program was that if it had existed prior to September, 11, 2001, it would have been possible to prevent the attack as the government would've been able to trace the hijackers.[49] Despite Rubio's claim being untrue at that time, it nevertheless does currently have a strong

---

[48] Available at: https://fas.org/irp/congress/2015_cr/050715-nsa.html
[49] Ibid.

foundation where he reflected that the government is not going through everyone's phone records;[50] prior to the passing of the USA Freedom Act that was exactly what was going on, but now the USA Freedom Act banned such a conduct by the NSA.

Ultimately, the aforementioned statements could be seen as lacking evidence, in addition to being filled with hope in their opposition to the ACLU ruling. According to Senator McConnell, "had these authorities been in place more than a decade ago, they would likely have prevented 9/11. … There has not been a single incident -- not one -- of an intentional abuse of them…" [51] On another note, and according to the former Director of the National Security Agency and the Former Commander of the United States Cyber Command Keith B. Alexander, "The programs assist the intelligence community to connect the dots."[52] Alexander further reflected that the NSA programs, both section 215 of the USA PATRIOT Act and section 702 of FISA, are legitimate counterterror tools and that such programs have helped disrupt at least ten plots involving terrorism suspects or targets in the

---

[50] Ibid.

[51] Ibid.

[52] Liz Klimas, NSA Director says spy programs helped stop 50 'potential terrorist attacks' - and gives two new examples, The Blaze (June 18, 2013), http://www.theblaze.com/news/2013/06/18/nsa-director-says-spy-programs-helped-stop-50-potential-terrorist-attacks-and-gives-two-new-examples/

United States.[53] In addition, with the passage of the USA Freedom Act that ended the bulk collection of data, Congress's intention was to assist the government in combating terrorism. As the USA Freedom Act was recently passed, the government requires more time to report to Congress the efficiency of the new amendments to the program. Nevertheless, the below paragraphs are to argue against the claims made above and are supported by experts with relevant expertise in intelligence.

According to the ACLU, between 2003 and 2005 fifty-three reported criminal referrals to prosecutors were made by the FBI as a result of 143,074 National Security Letters [54] and not a single letter was for terrorism.[55] Also, between the years 2003 and 2006, the FBI issued 192,499 NSLs, which led to one terror-related conviction.[56] Although the Justice Department's Inspector General Michael E. Horowitz stated that the data

---

[53] Elena Nakashima, Officials: Surveillance programs foiled more than 50 terrorist plots, The Washington Post (June 18, 2013),
https://www.washingtonpost.com/world/national-security/officials-surveillance-programs-foiled-more-than-50-terrorist-plots/2013/06/18/d657cb56-d83e-11e2-9df4-895344c13c30_story.html?utm_term=.4c029f0de562
[54] National Security Letters are issued by the FBI, without a judge's approval, to obtain personal information.
[55] A review of the FBI's Use of National Security Letters: Assessment of Corrective Actions and Examination of NSL Usage in 2006, U.S. Department of Justice: Office of the Inspector General (March 2008),
https://oig.justice.gov/special/s0803b/final.pdf
[56] Surveillance under the PATRIOT Act, ACLU. Available at:
https://www.aclu.org/infographic/surveillance-under-patriot-act

gathered by agents was valuable, they nevertheless only developed leads in other related criminal cases, not leads of terrorism plots.[57] Thus, the numbers reflect that the program did not make a concrete difference, probably due to the abuse of power by not employing the program in a correct manner, or the program's lack of efficiency in the first place.

In addition, The President's Review Group on Intelligence and Communications Technologies,[58] on December 12, 2013, reported that although surveillance programs can indeed protect from certain acts of terrorism and espionage, as well as protecting national security, there should nevertheless be proper control of the intelligence methods that serve in the nation's best interest. In relation to whether section 215 of the USA PATRIOT Act has been effective in preventing attacks, the Review Group stated that, "the information contributed to terrorist investigations by the use of section 215 telephony

---

[57] Maggie Ybarra, FBI admits no major cases cracked with Patriot Act snooping powers, The Washington Post (May 21, 2015),
http://www.washingtontimes.com/news/2015/may/21/fbi-admits-patriot-act-snooping-powers-didnt-crack/

[58] The President's Review Group was formed following the global surveillance disclosures by Snowden in 2013. This report was produced by a five-member group following Obama's instructions to assess whether, in light of the technological advancements, the United States employs its technical collection capabilities in a manner that protects national security and serves America's foreign policy. This was their final report as directed by Obama.

meta-data was not essential to preventing attacks and could readily have been obtained in a timely manner using conventional section 215 orders." [59] The Group ultimately stresses on the fact that advanced technological skills belonging to the intelligence community have a vital role in preventing and obstructing terrorism as well as identifying potential vulnerabilities in space.

Furthermore, the Privacy and Civil Liberties Board (PCLOB), which is an independent agency within the Executive Branch established by Congress in 2014, released its first report on January 23, 2014, reviewing Section 215 of the USA PATRIOT Act in response to the Snowden revelations.[60] In relation to the then NSA-run program of bulk collection under section 215, PCLOB's report on mass surveillance in 2014 found that little evidence exists that the section 215 program had actually yielded material results related to counterterrorism that could not have been achieved if it was not for the section 215 program.[61] PCLOB further provided that they are unaware,

---

[59] The President's Review Group on Intelligence and Communications Technologies, Liberty and Security in a Changing World, page 104 (2013)
[60] Report available at: https://www.pclob.gov/library/215-report_on_the_telephone_records_program.pdf
[61] Privacy and Civil Liberties Oversight Board, Report on the Telephone Records Program Conducted under Section 215 of the USA PATRIOT Act and on the Operations of the Foreign Intelligence Surveillance Court, page 146 (2014)

based on the information they received regarding the program and classified briefings and documentation, of any instances in which the program contributed to the discovery of unknown terrorist cells or the disruption of a terrorist attack.[62]

With regards to the above mentioned statement by former Director of the National Security Agency and the Former Commander of the United States Cyber Command, Keith B. Alexander, that the surveillance programs have helped disrupt at least 10 terror incidents,[63] we are to portray one of these incidents and demonstrate how section 215 had limited value and its lack of direct attribution to the program. One of those incidents involved David Coleman Headley, a former informant for the Drug Enforcement Agency. In 2013, Headley was sentenced to thirty-five years in prison for his role in the India 2008 Mumbai hotel attack and Denmark Terror plots, for plotting to attack the headquarters on the Danish Newspaper that published satire cartoons of Prophet Mohammed.[64] The

---

[62] Ibid.

[63] Elena Nakashima, Officials: Surveillance programs foiled more than 50 terrorist plots, The Washington Post (June 18, 2013), https://www.washingtonpost.com/world/national-security/officials-surveillance-programs-foiled-more-than-50-terrorist-plots/2013/06/18/d657cb56-d83e-11e2-9df4-895344c13c30_story.html?utm_term=.4c029f0de562

[64] David Coleman Headley Sentenced to 35 Years in Prison for Role in India and Denmark Terror Plots, Department of Justice: Office of Public Affairs (Jan 24, 2013), https://www.justice.gov/opa/pr/david-coleman-headley-sentenced-35-

PCLOB report provided that Headley was identified by law enforcement as involved in terrorism through other means that did not involve section 215, and his activities oversees were also identified without using section 215.[65] Finally, despite the NSA querying the call records via section 215 before passing them to the FBI, the numbers provided only corroborated data that the FBI acquired through other law enforcement agencies.[66]

PCLOB's report thus reflected that the program did not actually make the nation safer. Although PCLOB did not criticise the conduct of the NSA, they stressed that with the complexity of technology and with the bulk collection of data, there exists a potential for governmental abuse. Nevertheless, with the USA Freedom Act ending the bulk collection of data, which was recommended by PCLOB in their report and later mentioned in their Recommendations Assessment Report,[67] there may actually be instances where the program could be successful in locating terrorist cells or potential attacks due to the focus generated by the limited amount of data, which was actually

years-prison-role-india-and-denmark-terror-plots

[65] Privacy and Civil Liberties Oversight Board, Report on the Telephone Records Program Conducted under Section 215 of the USA PATRIOT Act and on the Operations of the Foreign Intelligence Surveillance Court, page 151 (2014)

[66] Ibid.

[67] Privacy and Civil Liberties Oversight Board, Recommendations Assessment Report, page 2 (2016)

requested directly from the communication providers. Ultimately, as the metadata may be queried only when there is an RAS, based on articulated facts, the NSA will avoid the general browsing of the data as it can only obtain records of calls up to two hops from the enquired number, which may thus lead to increased reliability in locating terrorist cells or potential attacks. As mentioned earlier, The USA Freedom Act bans the bulk collection of data - three hop proves - and in doing so the Act authorized the government to collect data from phone companies up to 'two hops' of communicants records related to a suspect. This is dependent upon the government providing evidence that it has an RAS that the suspect is linked with a terrorist organization. This will be portrayed in more depth in the following paragraphs.

The aforementioned definition of 'terrorism' under the USA PATRIOT Act is quite broad, and should be narrowed down, or else the authority that will flow from that definition could become abusive, as it is reflected from the argument. Additionally, it could lead to government authorization of the seizure or conduction of surveillance on any person belonging to a certain group, or even ethnicity, as long as that person is merely pointed out as a possible suspect. Ultimately, in reviewing the section 215 program, no evidence exists that the collection of data has provided any valuable intelligence that could not have been gathered through other means.

Although the USA Freedom Act introduced changes related to the method and quantity of collection of data to the section 215 surveillance program, but can the Act be considered a victory for privacy rights advocates? It would be appropriate to quote Jameel Jaffer, the ACLU's deputy legal director, as he stated that although the Act is a milestone, it still leaves too many of the overbroad government surveillance powers in place.[68] For instance, although metadata does not include the name, address, or financial information of any telephone customer, it can still reveal intimate details about a person's life, particularly after carrying out the second hop. Thus, it can be said that the section 215 program does indeed have serious implications with regards to privacy. Hence, the below points will elaborate further on the privacy concerns that still prevail and how the USA PATRIOT Act, specifically section 215, has generated a great deal of concern since its enactment. Nevertheless, those processes all allow the NSA to identify any concerns early in the process to minimize the adverse impact on privacy. Here we are to elaborate on the

---

[68] Senate Passes USA Freedom Act, ACLU (June 2, 2015), https://www.aclu.org/news/senate-passes-usa-freedom-act

minimization procedures and transparency of the operation of section 215.

In relation to the minimization procedures under section 215 of the USA PATRIOT Act, there would be stricter critique of the entire procedure if not for the amendments introduced by the USA Freedom Act in 2015. Hence, with those amendments in place, section 215 may actually be in a position where it protects civil liberties and the privacy of individuals, yet it still has its flaws. Section 4 of Presidential Policy Directive 28 - Safeguarding Personal Information Collected through Signals Intelligence - is of relevance here as it provides a clarification of the minimization procedures.[69] Hence, and as reflected from the text of PPD 28, the Director of National Intelligence as well as the Attorney General will ensure that the intelligence community establishes policies that apply the minimization procedures under PPD 28 to protect personal information collected from signals intelligence activities (SIGINT). In addition, section 4 of PPD 28 makes strong reference to E.O. 12333 - probably because they are both orders issued by the

---

[69] PPD 28. Section 4. Safeguarding Personal Information Collected through Signals Intelligence "U.S. signals intelligence activities must, therefore, include appropriate safeguards for the personal information of all individuals, regardless of the nationality of the individual to whom the information pertains or where that individual resides."

President of the United States – and thus both articulate the executive branch's national security policy 'not overruled yet' and have the effect of law. In portraying the implementation of the minimization procedures, we are to elaborate on the dissemination and the retention of call records. Thus, it ought to be considered whether the dissemination and retention of data procedures under section 215 of the USA PATRIOT Act fall into that category. In addition, pursuant to 50 U.S. Code. 1861. g (1)(2a), it should be considered whether the procedures under section 215 are reasonably designed to fit the Attorney General document of 'minimization procedures'.

Furthermore, in order to ensure that proper privacy safeguards and civil liberties are in place, and in response to Section 4 of the Presidential Policy Directive 28 (PPD-28), which articulates principles to guide the United States' conduct in relation to SIGINT activities for authorized foreign intelligence and counterintelligence purposes,[70] the NSA worked with the Whitehouse in developing policies and procedures for safeguarding personal data collected during signal intelligence (SIGINT) activities, which ultimately led to the NSA establishing the United States Signals Intelligence Directive

---

[70] Available at: https://obamawhitehouse.archives.gov/the-press-office/2014/01/17/presidential-policy-directive-signals-intelligence-activities

SP0018. It is vital to stress that PPD 28 emphasizes the fact that sharing personal data is essential to protecting national security, and the United States takes privacy concerns into account by setting appropriate limits on such sharing.

In relation to 'USSID 18', once the NSA has identified the information it finds relevant to its counterterrorism investigations, it passes said information to other federal agencies.[71] Hence, taking into consideration that USSID 18 prescribes policies and minimization procedures to ensure that the missions of the United States signal intelligence system are conducted in a manner that protects the privacy rights of U.S. citizens, the NSA must apply section 7 of USSID 18 when sharing phone records with other agencies. Section 7 of USSID 18 delineates the rules for the dissemination of information related to U.S. individuals to ensure the protection of individual privacy.

As a safeguard against the overbroad collection of data, section 101 (b)(vii)(I) of the USA Freedom Act requires the government to "adopt minimization procedures calling for the prompt destruction of all call detail records" that are

---

[71] USSID 18. Available at;
https://www.dni.gov/files/documents/1118/CLEANEDFinal USSID SP0018.pdf

determined not to be foreign intelligence related.[72] On November 24, 2015, Attorney General of the United States, Loretta E. Lynch, signed the document 'minimization procedures used by the national security agency in connection with the production of call detail records pursuant to section 501 of FISA, as amended.'[73] This document sets out the most up to date 'minimization procedures' that apply to the retention and dissemination of call detail records. Hence, in order for NSA personnel to be able to disseminate the data acquired under section 215 of the USA PATRIOT Act, they must act in accordance with the requirements of the procedures set by the Attorney General.

In recapping the dissemination and retention of call records under section 215 of the USA PATRIOT Act; when the NSA identifies communications that may be associated with terrorism, intelligence reports are issued to other federal agencies to work on preventing such attacks. Hence, the FBI can use such data obtained from the NSA to investigate terrorist operatives and terrorist threats inside the United States. In adhering to certain minimization procedures that govern the manner in which this metadata may be used within the NSA

---

[72] USA Freedom Act of 2015. Section 101 (b)(vii)(I)

[73] Available at: https://www.nsa.gov/about/civil-liberties/reports/assets/files/UFA_SMPs_Nov_2015.pdf

and disseminated outside of it, the NSA ought to adhere to the various, yet spread out, minimization requirements required by the FISA Court in its different 'Primary Orders.'[74] In addition, the following paragraphs, portraying the minimization procedures that govern the dissemination and retention of call records, are a reflection of the Attorney General's document for the protection of call records under section 215. Hence, the following paragraphs contain the minimization procedures that govern the manner in which the NSA can disseminate and retain the data it obtains to other agencies within the intelligence community.

The first step includes obtaining the phone records where the FBI (on behalf of the NSA) may file an application with the Foreign Intelligence Surveillance Court.[75] Upon receiving the application, members of the FISC's legal staff review the request and evaluate whether the application meets the legal

---

[74] Privacy and Civil Liberties Oversight Board, Report on the Telephone Records Program Conducted under Section 215 of the USA PATRIOT Act and on the Operations of the Foreign Intelligence Surveillance Court, page 23 (2014) "When the FISA court approves the government's applications to renew the program, the Court issues a "primary order" outlining the scope of what each telephone company must furnish to the NSA and the conditions under which the government can use, retain, and disseminate the data."

[75] Although it is the FBI that is requesting the call records, as requested by section 215, but they typically note that they are requesting them for the NSA. Thus, the FISC's orders direct the corporations to provide the records to the 'NSA.'

requirements under FISA. Thus, providing an independent judicial check at the beginning of any potential request as they identify flaws in the government's statuary and constitutional analysis.

The second step involves selecting the seed. Prior to using a specific phone number as the target or the seed, for a query, one of twenty-two designated NSA officials, as well as one of the two senior analyst officials, must determine and approve that there is a reasonable, articulable suspicion (RAS) that the number is associated with terrorism. Additionally, if the selection term can be reasonably believed to be used by a U.S. person, the number may not be regarded as associated with terrorism solely on the basis of activities protected by the First Amendment. The RAS standard has been characterized by Government officials as the cornerstone minimization procedure as it ensures the overall reasonableness of the program.[76] Hence, the purpose of the RAS method is to prevent any general browsing of the data by officials. After the seed has been selected, it is only valid for one year, or six months if reasonably believed to be a U.S. citizen. Ultimately, the seed

---

[76] In re Application of the Federal Bureau of Investigation for an Order Requiring the Production of Tangible Things, No. BR 09-09 (FISA Ct. Aug. 17, 2009).

provides the basis from which the NSA can obtain the metadata.

The third step concerns the query process that is dependent on the FISC's permission to initiate the investigation. A query is a search for a specific number or another selection term within the database. The amendments brought by the USA Freedom Act had a vital impact in this process, hence, instead of the bulk collection of data - the three hop process, the USA Freedom Act limited the query process to two hops. Thus, the government can collect up to two hops [77] of call records related to a suspect as long as it can prove that there is a 'RAS' that the target is linked to a terrorist or espionage organization. Ultimately, if the acquired number belongs to a U.S. person, and prior to disseminating the data outside the agency, one of five high level NSA officials must determine whether the data is related to counterterrorism information and whether the data is necessary for countering terrorism. However, although the FBI has certain minimization procedures set forth in the Attorney General's Guidelines for Domestic FBI Operations,[78] the FISA Court has not established any minimization

---

[77] Those hops are also known as 'contact chaining' which is the process of identifying the connections among individuals via their phone calls.
[78] Available at: https://www.justice.gov/archive/opa/docs/guidelines.pdf

procedures for how other federal agencies should handle information received from the NSA.

To further elaborate on both the minimization procedure relating to the dissemination and retention of the call records, and taking section 7 of USSID 18 into consideration, the NSA - as previously stated - prior to sharing the data with other agencies, should apply the minimization procedures set forth under Section 7 of the USSID 18. As can be seen from the steps through which the NSA obtains data, and by taking USSID 18 into consideration, we have come to the following findings. The rules prescribed by USSID 18, section 7, seem to be broad in their scope, which may create some sort of weakness in protecting the privacy of U.S. persons. For instance, under 7.2, the conditions of including the identification of U.S. persons in signal intelligence reports go on for three pages, which does not make such inclusion in reports by the IC that challenging. Nevertheless, we have found that the intent and the direction of USSID 18 is clear, due to it being followed by the intelligence community. Similarly, section 2.3 of E.O. 12333 contains an absurd amount of exceptions whereby agencies are permitted to collect, disseminate, and retain data belonging to U.S. persons. Hence, ten exceptions are outlined that could easily be taken an advantage of, such as '(j) information necessary for administrative purposes,' raising the question of what would constitute necessity? This is not only vague, but also too broad, which may open the door for abuse and mishandling by the intelligence community.

In relation to the retention of data, the NSA - as previously stated - stores the data in a centralized database where NSA analysts are permitted to access the section 215 records only through queries of the database. As a safeguard, only one of twenty-two NSA officials must first determine the existence of a RAS that the number could be related to terrorism. In addition, when the NSA receives the call records, such records are stored in repositories within secure networks under the NSA's control, and after the data is housed within the NSA repositories, only technical and trained personnel can then take additional measures to implement the records for intelligence purposes. Hence, access to those records is restricted, as only those who have received adequate training can access the data for analysis.

Although it appears from the text that the NSA has actually been adhering to the principles and rules governing the dissemination and retention of call records, several missteps and complaints still exist. The NSA should avoid violating the general applicable rules governing the NSA's activities, such as the USSID 18, PPD 28, E.O. 12333, and the Attorney General's latest recommendations. Nevertheless, the aforementioned safeguards outlined in the previous paragraphs, relating to both the dissemination and retention of data under section 215, demonstrate that with the passage of the USA Freedom Act- ending the Bulk collection of data, two hop process, and retention of data by corporations, - and the continuing amendments to FISC's primary orders, and with PCLOB's successful recommendations[79], section 215 of the USA PATRIOT Act is certainly in a better position than it was prior to June 2, 2015.

After the Snowden Leaks, the NSA was casted a critical look by the general public as it began to question the NSA's operation under a broad spectrum with too few safeguards, creating a balance between national security and personal privacy. However, when discussing the aforementioned points relating to the minimization requirements provided by PPDD

---

[79] Privacy and Civil Liberties Oversight Board, Report on the Telephone Records Program Conducted under Section 215 of the USA PATRIOT Act and on the Operations of the Foreign Intelligence Surveillance Court, page 16 (2014) "Recommendation 1: The Government should end its section 215 bulk telephone records program.

28, E.O. 12333, Attorney General, and USSID 18, it ought to be stated that section 215 of the USA PATRIOT Act is progressing towards more adequate privacy protections due to the restrictions imposed by the 2015 USA Freedom Act and the continuous amendments by the FISC's Primary Orders. Ultimately, the minimization procedures could be portrayed as including appropriate safeguards for the personal data of U.S. persons. Considering that the sharing of such information between agencies of the U.S. intelligence community is essential to the protection of national security, at the same time appropriate limits on such sharing are set, which thus reflects that the United States takes the privacy concerns into account under section 215 of the USA PATRIOT Act.

Transparency is one of the foundations of democratic governance as it supports accountability and is vital to governmental activities that affect individual rights. In relation to the transparency of section 215 by both the government and private entities, we ought to mention that secrecy may actually be required to a certain extent, as we would not want enemies to comprehend the capabilities of applied intelligence. Nevertheless, openness or transparency is also vital to being more informed and aware about the exercise of collection authorities, which can actually increase public confidence in the intelligence process. The issue here is that the public is unaware of the scope of section 215 surveillance, the opinions of the FISC, and disclosure by private entities regarding government requests. As James Madison observed, "A popular Government, without popular information, or the means of acquiring it, is but a Prologue to a Farce or a Tragedy; or, perhaps both."[80]

To initiate this discussion, it is vital to mention a relevant document that was published to directly address the intelligence community in relation to the 'Transparency' issue, as directed by President Obama. On February 2015, the Director of National Intelligence published 'The Principles of Intelligence Transparency Implementation Plan' in order to enhance the public understanding of activities conducted by the intelligence community.[81] This document was made available to enhance public understanding of intelligence activities in general, as well as to protect personal information when such disclosures would harm national security. Although the rules or

---

[80] Office of Information Policy, Celebrating James Madison and the Freedom of Information Act, The United Sates Department of Justice (Mar 13, 2008), https://www.justice.gov/oip/blog/foia-post-2008-celebrating-james-madison-and-freedom-information-act
Letter from James Madison to W.T. Barry (Aug. 4, 1822) in The Writings of James Madison
[81] Office of the Director of National Intelligence, Principles of Intelligence Transparency: Implementation Plan, (2015)

principles examined in this document do not supersede existing laws and executive orders, but they articulate general rules that the different agencies in the intelligence community are advised to implement. According to the document there are four principles. First, provide appropriate transparency to enhance public understanding of the intelligence conducted. Second, be proactive and clear in making information publicly available. Third, protect information about intelligence sources, methods, and activities. Fourth, align the agency's roles, resources, processes, and policies to support transparency implementation. It will be examined whether those principles have been met under the amended version of section 215 of the USA PATRIOT Act, as they are intended to facilitate the intelligence community's decision on making information public.

In relation to the transparency related to the functioning of section 215, in June 2013 following the Snowden revelations of the Guardian, it has been revealed that the Bush and Obama administrations had been secretly using section 215 of the USA PATRIOT Act to acquire call records of Americans in bulk. In the aftermath, the government released a substantial amount of information to inform the public on governmental surveillance programs. For instance, the Obama administration was forced to explain to the German Chancellor Angela Merkel the U.S. spying. Hence, the United States was in a questionable situation, both locally and globally.

When section 215 of the USA PATRIOT Act was adopted in 2001 - only 45 days following the September 11 attacks - it was debated by various privacy advocate groups, such as the Electronic Privacy Information Centre[82] and the American Civil Liberties Union,[83] that the Bill in general was adopted and passed with great haste, with little debate, and without a Senate, House, or Conference report. Thus, the Act, at that time, lacked any legislative history which is necessary when statuary interpretation is needed. This was due to the September, 11, 2001, terror attacks, which convinced majorities in Congress that national law officials need new and immediate legal tools to combat terrorism. Nevertheless, following the Snowden disclosures in 2013, Congress believed that the public's trust in the intelligence community needed to be restored, thus the USA Freedom Act was passed and the bulk collection of data as well as the three hop query process were all ended. Unlike section 215 of the USA PATRIOT Act, the USA Freedom Act

---

[82] USA Patriot Act, epic.org. available at:
https://epic.org/privacy/terrorism/usapatriot/
[83] Susan N. Herman, The USA PATRIOT Act and the Submajoritarian Fourth Amendment, 41 Harvard Civil Right-Civil Liberties Law Review. 61 (2006)

has been extensively debated since October 2013 until Congress passed it on June 2, 2015.

Although Congress was under pressure to pass the USA Freedom Act due to several provisions of the USA PATRIOT Act expiring on May 31, 2015, it renewed these provisions in a more limited form as well as placing measures on the collection of phone records belonging to Americans. Ultimately, between 2013 and 2015, the USA Freedom Act was debated extensively by Congress as well as by civil liberties group where the debate was focused on the best way to end the bulk collection of phone records. Thus, with the pressure on Congress and the intelligence community in the years following the Snowden revelations, it can be said that the collection of phone records belonging to Americans was accompanied with public debate that aimed to best serve policies affecting the privacy rights of Americans.

Furthermore, as the Snowden revelations led Congress to significantly curtail domestic bulk collection of phone records in 2015 by passing the USA Freedom Act, it also led to the Act containing reform provisions, such as disclosures by the private sector on National Security Letters (NSLs).[84] NSLs

---

[84] USA Freedom Act. Section 502

can be described as a search procedure that gives the FBI authority to demand corporations to hand over certain customer records. These corporations are prohibited from telling anyone about their receipt of an NSL. They are also known as a 'gag orders.' Those gag orders had an adverse effect on individual privacy whereby documents such as financial records, credit information, and even telephone and email records were being demanded. The FBI was then able to gain corporation to hand over sensitive information about innocent people, which can be considered an example of legal authority significantly expanding the universe of information with a letter that was not obtained via a court order. In summary, the USA PATRIOT Act prohibited Americans and corporations who received NSLs from telling anyone as a 'gag order.'

However, after the passage of the USA Freedom Act, and pursuant to Tile VI, section 604, private corporations or individuals were granted the right to disclose National Security Letters received. Also, the government was required to issue more public reports on such orders. In addition, The President's Review Group on Intelligence and Communications Technologies in their 2013 report, 'Liberty and Security In a Changing World,' back in 2013, recommended that "legislation should be enacted requiring that detailed information about authorities such as those involving National Security Letters, section 215 business records…".[85] Thus, after the passage of the USA Freedom Act, corporations and individuals can now cite the Act as a legal justification for releasing such documents under section 604.[86]

Yahoo, Google, and Twitter are all examples of corporations publishing national security letters after the gag orders have been dropped. In relation to Yahoo, Yahoo became the first corporation to go public about the NSLs they had received without having to face the FBI in court. Yahoo disclosed that it received letters in 2013 and 2015, and in quoting Chris Madsen, Yahoo's head of global law enforcement, security and safety, "We believe this is an important step toward enriching a more open and transparent discussion about the legal authorities law enforcement can leverage to access user data."[87] Google is another global tech corporation that published on December 13, 2016, eight national security letters it received from the FBI.[88] In addition, Twitter joined the ranks of Yahoo,

---

[85]The President's Review Group on Intelligence and Communications Technologies, Liberty and Security in a Changing World, page 122 (201)
[86] USA Freedom Act. Title VI. Section 604.
[87] Kim Zetter, Yahoo publishes national security letters after FBI drops gag orders, WIRED (Jan 1, 2016), https://www.wired.com/2016/06/yahoo-publishes-national-security-letters-fbi-drops-gag-orders/
[88] Kate Conger, Google just published eight national security letters, techcrunch (Dec 13, 2016), https://techcrunch.com/2016/12/13/google-national-security-

Google, and other corporations earlier this year by announcing that it had received two NSLs, one in 2015 and the other in 2016.[89] Ultimately, the aforementioned corporations all stressed the fact that it is vital to take such orders to the public as they are issued without prior judicial oversight, and that the wealth of data includes personal information that should not be subjected to secret searches without the approval of a court.

With corporations publicly disclosing the total number of NSLs they had received, in addition to the number of individuals whose records have been requested, Congress and the American public are therefore being informed about the trend in the surveillance program. In addition, publicly disclosed reports by telecommunication or internet providers is vital to building and maintaining public trust. Ultimately, as private corporations may now periodically report the number of governmental inquiries, as well as the existence of oversight by Congress, the DoJ, and the FISC as provided by the USA Freedom Act, and the American public is thus provided with a clear idea of these inquiries. Thus, the extensive oversight due

---

letters/

[89] Kate Conger, Twitter releases national security letters, TechCrunch (Jan 27, 2017), https://techcrunch.com/2017/01/27/twitter-releases-national-security-letters/

to the nature of the inquiries should go a long way in protecting privacy and allaying the concern related.

Regardless of the criticisms provided, section 215 of the USA PATRIOT Act - especially after the amendments by the USA Freedom Act of banning the bulk collection of data and reducing the specific selection term of records down two hops from the enquired number - appears to have made significant strides in implementing the privacy safeguards that were lacking in its initial form prior to being amended in 2015.

In relation to transparency, and as reflected from the discussions, it could be argued that disclosures about government surveillance programs that involve the collection, dissemination, and retention of personal data relating to American individuals is possible without causing harm to national security. Even if the targets are not disclosed, the public is not kept in the dark but is actually informed of the processes, functions, and conducts that are carried out under section 215 of the USA PATRIOT Act, or under governmental surveillance programs in general. Yet, we should ask the question, would have those disclosures happened if it was not for the Snowden leaks?

However, the biggest criticisms here, as is with all the subsections discussed under section 215, is that there is a wide variety of recommendations, implementation plans, and legal authorities that produce the criteria of implementing such an issue, which thus causes confusion and damages the credibility of the intelligence community documents.

iii.   The Foreign Intelligence Surveillance Act of 1978. Section 702

Section 702 of the Foreign Intelligence Surveillance Act (FISA) is the third piece of law that we are to discuss in relation to surveillance by the United States government. Section 702 of FISA refers to part of the FISA Amendments Act of 2008 (FAA) which renewed the U.S. government's authority to monitor internet communications of foreigners outside the United States.[90] Hence, section 702 was a new provision added to FISA permitting the Attorney General and the Director of National Intelligence to authorize in a joint manner the targeting of communications of persons reasonably believed to be located outside the United States, solely for foreign intelligence purposes.[91] Such surveillance is conducted

---

[90] Associated Press. Congress extends surveillance law, POLITICO (Dec 28, 2012), http://www.pcworld.com/article/3180766/security/the-nsas-foreign-surveillance-5-things-to-kn

with the assistance of United States electronic communication service providers, such as Microsoft and Google, whereby the data is stored within the United States. Hence, the government is not permitted, under this program, to directly target any U.S. person located anywhere in the world, nor does it have the authority to target a person believed to be outside the U.S. in order to acquire information about another person inside the U.S.[92] Indeed, the current objective of the programs under section 702 is to thwart terrorist acts. Nevertheless, we shall analyse the other functions and safeguards of section 702 further on in this section.

In terms of how surveillance under section 702 is carried out, the Attorney General and the Director of National Intelligence submit annual certifications to the FISC that identify information or data related to foreign intelligence that may be collected.[93] Hence, unlike section 215 of the USA PATRIOT Act, section 702 does not require individual judicial orders from the Court for every target. In order for the certification to be approved by the FISC, it must demonstrate that the target is

---

[91] Foreign Intelligence Surveillance Act. Title VII, Section 702. 50. U.S.C. 1881a.
[92] Foreign Intelligence Surveillance Act. Title VII, Section 702 b (2) (3). 50. U.S.C. 1881a.
[93] Foreign Intelligence Surveillance Act. Title VII, Section 702 g (1). 50. U.S.C. 1881a.

'reasonably believed' to be located outside the United States, that the minimization and targeting procedures satisfy certain criteria,[94] and that the procedures are consistent with the 4th Amendment to the United States Constitution.

Once the FISC approves the acquisition under section 702, the Attorney General and the Director of National Intelligence may direct the electronic communication service provider to immediately provide the government with all that is necessary to accomplish the acquisition of communications.[95] Thus, after the acquisition of all the required information, such as telephone numbers and email addresses, the government selects certain 'targets' and sends them to the electronic communication service providers to begin acquisition. There are two types of acquisitions under section 702, PRISM and Upstream, which are to be displayed below.

In its fight against terrorism, the U.S. intelligence community has indicated section 702 as the 'most important tool.'[96] Indeed,

---

[94] Foreign Intelligence Surveillance Act. Title VII, Section 702 g (2). 50. U.S.C. 1881a.

[95] Foreign Intelligence Surveillance Act. Title VII, Section 702 h (1) (a). 50. U.S.C. 1881a.

[96] Grant Gross, The NSA's foreign surveillance: 5 things to know, PC WORLD (Mar 14, 2017), http://www.politico.com/story/2012/12/congress-extends-foreign-surveillance-law-085563ow.html

as section 702 authorizes foreign surveillance programs by the NSA like PRISM and Upstream it ought to be considered to be a critical tool in U.S. foreign surveillance.[97] PRISM and Upstream are both part of the Special Source Operations[98] in which they are responsible for collecting information and data by establishing a cooperative type of a relationship with corporations.[99] Briefly, under PRISM, the NSA acquires communications 'to' or 'from' a section 702 selector, such as an email address or a number. While under Upstream, the NSA acquires communications 'to', 'from', or 'about' a section 702 selector.

PRISM, also known as downstream collection, is a program in which the NSA operates substantial surveillance whereby extensive data mining efforts are utilized under section 702 of the FISA Amendments Act of 2008 (FAA) to collect and

---

[97] Both programs were revealed in 2013 by former NSA contractor Edward Snowden.

[98] Barton Gellman and Laura Poitras, U.S., British intelligence mining data from nine U.S. Internet companies in broad secret program, The Washington Post (June 7, 2013), https://www.washingtonpost.com/investigations/us-intelligence-mining-data-from-nine-us-internet-companies-in-broad-secret-program/2013/06/06/3a0c0da8-cebf-11e2-8845-d970ccb04497_story.html?utm_term=.c92b23a07f00

[99] Ewan Macakill and Gabriel Dance, NSA Files: Decoded, The Guardian (November 1, 2013), https://www.theguardian.com/world/interactive/2013/nov/01/snowden-nsa-files-surveillance-revelations-decoded - section/1

analyse information for terrorist patterns. The basic idea behind the PRISM program is that it allows the NSA to obtain information and data from the servers of at least nine major internet companies such as Google, Facebook, Yahoo, Microsoft, and others.[100] Here, the government sends a selector, such as an email address or phone number, to a U.S. based internet service provider (ISP) and the service provider is thus compelled to forward the communication 'to' and 'from' related to that selector to the government. The NSA, the CIA and the FBI each may receive data under PRISM. As the program collects videos, photos, e-mails, or even chats, it has been indicated by NSA documents - revealed by Snowden - that PRISM is "the number one source of raw intelligence used for NSA analytic reports."[101] Ultimately, the PRISM program falls under the jurisdiction of the FISC and can only collect data after been given permission by the FISC. According to the Director of U.S. National Intelligence, "PRISM is operated under strict supervision and cannot be used to intentionally target any Americans or anyone in the United States." [102]

---

[100] Glen Greenwald and Ewen MacAskill, NSA Prism program taps in to user data of Apple, Google and others, The Guardian (June 7, 2013), https://www.theguardian.com/world/2013/jun/06/us-tech-giants-nsa-data
[101] The Washington Post, NSA slides explain the PRISM data collection program, The News-Herald (June 7, 2013), http://www.news-herald.com/article/HR/20130607/NEWS/306079994
[102] House Select Intelligence Committee Holds Hearing on Disclosure of National Security Agency Surveillance Programs (June 18, 2013), available at:

Upstream collection is another NSA surveillance program, which involves the NSA's interception of both telephone and Internet traffic by tapping Internet cables and switches. This involves tapping undersea fibre-optic cables, which means that the NSA is associated with providers that control the telecommunications backbone, not with service providers such as Internet corporations. The NSA's collection of communications includes both their metadata and content, and from major domestic and foreign internet cables and switches, hence, the internet backbone. Under this program, only the NSA is entitled to receive data. Generally, Upstream collection is conducted under the following major surveillance programs; Fairview, Blarney, Oakstar, and Stormbrew; and under each program a different type of filtering is carried out.[103] For instance, Fairview, Blarney, and Stormbrew are responsible for collecting data at facilities within the United States, and the programs under the Oakstar umbrella intercept communication in facilities outside the United States.[104] Thus, under the

---

https://www.eff.org/files/2015/04/29/alexanderselectintelcommittee_06182013_p5p60p61.pdf

[103] Siobhan Gorman and Jennifer Valentino-DeVries, NSA Surveillance Programs Cover 75% of Internet Traffic Transiting U.S., The Wall Street Journal (Aug 21, 2013), http://www.matthewaid.com/post/58904880659/nsa-surveillance-programs-cover-75-of-internet

[104] As portrayed by the NSA slides leaked by Snowden. Available at: http://2.bp.blogspot.com/-

aforementioned programs, the collection of information or data occurs both inside and outside the United States. It is worth mentioning that the aforementioned four programs had been initially disclosed by the Brazilian media in 2013 where unpublished PowerPoint slides relating to NSA operations were provided to the media by Snowden, and later published by The New York Times in 2015.[105] As will be shown below, upstream collection includes two features; the acquisition of 'about' communications, and the acquisition of 'multiple communications transactions' (MTC).

> *"...An "about" communication is one in which the selector of a targeted person (such as that person's email address) is contained within the communication but the targeted person is not necessarily a participant in the communication. Rather than being "to" or "from" the selector that has been tasked, the communication may contain the selector in the body of the communication, and thus be "about" the selector.*

---

nKB2vKKtCgQ/UlnHUKcNQVI/AAAAAAAAAx4/sPBlANBkPdc/s1600/cableta p-10-corpport.jpg

[105] Julia Angwin, Charlie Savage, Jeff Larson, Henrik Moltke, Laura Poitras, and James Risen, AT&T Helped U.S. Spy on Internet on a Vast Scale, The New York Times (Aug 15, 2015), https://www.nytimes.com/2015/08/16/us/politics/att-helped-nsa-spy-on-an-array-of-internet-traffic.html

An MCT is an Internet "transaction" that contains more than one discrete communication within it. If one of the communications within an MCT is to, from, or "about" a tasked selector, and if one end of the transaction is foreign, the NSA will acquire the entire MCT through upstream collection, including other discrete communications within the MCT that do not contain the selector." [106]

Nevertheless, unlike section 215 of the USA PATRIOT Act that was subject to amendment by the USA Freedom Act - the ban on the domestic bulk collection of communication records, - surveillance programs under section 702 of FISA were left untouched by the USA Freedom Act. The USA Freedom Act enacted preliminary limits only in relation to domestic phone surveillance, while leaving the internet unprotected. Although section 702 programs are ostensibly targeted at foreigners, they nonetheless collect a vast amount of information and data related to American persons during the process. The documents leaked by Snowden revealed that section 702 was "being used far more heavily than many

---

[106] Privacy and Civil Liberties Oversight Board, Report on the Surveillance Program Operated Pursuant to Section 702 of the Foreign Intelligence Surveillance Act, Page 7 (2014)

expected, serving as the legal basis for the collection of large quantities of telephone and Internet traffic." [107]

In relation to whether the privacy of American persons is actually protected under section 702, one of the biggest issues involves the way in which communications are treated by the surveillance programs. To recap, although section 702 only permits collection of information or data belonging to foreign persons oversees, privacy advocates within the United States nevertheless worry that large quantities of data belonging to American persons are being swept 'incidentally' and then used as well. This is known as incidental collection as well as backdoor search, which occurs when U.S. residents communicate with foreign targets who are subject to NSA surveillance. As 'incidental' collection happens by design, it is questionable whether it is actually incidental. In quoting Representative Conyers Jr, a Michigan Democrat, "This collection of U.S. communications without a warrant is, "in a word, wrong."[108]

---

[107] FISA: 702 Collection, Lawfare, https://www.lawfareblog.com/topic/fisa-702-collection

[108] Statement at the March 1, 2017, meeting that addressed the Foreign Intelligence Surveillance Act amendments that are set to expire by the end of the year unless action is taken by Congress.

In addition, when quantifying the number of incidental collections under the section 702 programs, neither the Officer of the Director of National Intelligence nor any agency in the government could give an estimate. Nevertheless, after the Snowden revelations, the Washington post, depending on raw intelligence material, found that, "ninety percent of communications collected under Section 702 were not the intended surveillance targets but were caught in a net the agency had cast for somebody else."[109] It is thus apparent that the large scale surveillance potential under section 702 has led to many Americans having their communications swept up or even used by intelligence agencies.[110]

So where are the loopholes that exist here? As the surveillance is warrantless, and the FISC does not review the government's individual targeting decisions, and the government is thus not required to show that it has a suspicion that a specific person has engaged in any wrongdoing. In addition, and under section

---

[109] Available at: https://www.washingtonpost.com/world/national-security/in-nsa-intercepted-data-those-not-targeted-far-outnumber-the-foreigners-who-are/2014/07/05/8139adf8-045a-11e4-8572-4b1b969b6322_story.html?utm_term=.e622d051bda8

[110] For instance, the incidental collection of U.S. citizens involved in the Trump transition period. Details about the U.S. persons who were involved were widely disseminated. House Intelligence Committee Chairman Devin Nunes. Available at: http://www.newsweek.com/its-not-just-trump-we-are-all-victims-incidental-collection-574776

702, the government can seize the data as long as it is significantly believed to be for foreign intelligence information, not solely for terrorism purposes.[111] Thus, 'foreign intelligence purposes' is such an expansive term that could have multiple sets of purposes, as well as it encompassing any information relevant to the foreign affairs of the U.S. In addition, James Clapper, former Director of National Intelligence, admitted to using the 'backdoor search' loophole which allowed for searches involving data and information belonging to American persons when the data was swept.[112] Ultimately, as the government is not allowed to target U.S. persons directly, nor reverse target,[113] it may hope to pick up someone thought to be in the United States when picking a foreign target.

Ultimately, as reflected under section 702, there is no requirement that the government demonstrates that there is an RAS of terrorist activity for the acquisition of information or data. Thus, the only criteria put in place under section 702 for the acquisition of information and data is that included in the

---

[111] Foreign Intelligence Surveillance Act. Title VII, Section 702 (a). 50. U.S.C. 1881a.

[112] Claire Mullican, Section 702's Expiration Date -- Could it Bring Backdoor Searches to an End?, Freedom Works (April 8, 2017), http://www.freedomworks.org/content/section-702%E2%80%99s-expiration-date-could-it-bring-backdoor-searches-end

[113] The targeting of a U.S. person under the guise or pretext of targeting a foreigner.

Act itself, which is that the acquisition must be for foreign intelligence purposes.

On April 28, 2017, the NSA announced that it will be putting an end to the 'about' collection feature under the upstream program of section 702. In quoting the Agency, "After considerable evaluation of the program and available technology, NSA has decided that its Section 702 foreign intelligence surveillance activities will no longer include any upstream internet communications that are solely "about" a foreign intelligence target."[114] This decision came after the NSA conducted a comprehensive review and evaluation of the privacy interests of United States persons, and it was discovered that NSA analysts violated rules imposed by the FISC barring any searching of information of American persons captured through surveillance. Thus, the NSA's surveillance, under upstream, will only be limited to those communications 'to' or 'from' a foreign intelligence selector. In addition to halting the 'about' collection of data, the NSA stated that it will take steps as soon as it is practicable to delete the vast majority of data collected under upstream.[115]

---

[114] NSA, NSA Stops certain Section 702 "Upstream" Activities, Statement (April 28, 2017), https://www.nsa.gov/news-features/press-room/statements/2017-04-28-702-statement.shtml

[115] Ibid.

Nevertheless, this curtailment is not considered an appropriate safeguard by all privacy advocates, for instance, Guliani, American Civil Liberties Union legislative counsel, reflected that although this action by the NSA will curb some abuses under FISA, it is merely a partial fix.[116]

Therefore, could the NSA's decision to no longer conduct 'about' searches serve in providing additional protections for the privacy of U.S. persons seeing as section 702's net is so large and inaccurate that information belonging to Americans was caught in the process of collecting foreign intelligence information? Or has this all been a ploy by the NSA to prevent Congress from terminating the entire section when it is up for reauthorization at the end of this year? Ultimately, regardless of its reasons, the NSA will certainly lose a lot of data due to the halting of 'about' collection, yet, the agency clearly seeks to reduce the chances of it inadvertently collecting information belonging to American persons. This is certainly a necessary step towards the right direction of protecting the privacy of Americans.

---

[116] ACLU, NSA Ends controversial surveillance practice (April 28, 2017), https://www.aclu.org/news/nsa-ends-controversial-surveillance-practice

In describing whether section 702 is reasonably designed to protect the privacy of Americans while considering legitimate national security interests, we are to analyse the minimization procedures and targeting requirements related to section 702. The below paragraphs will describe the ways by which the NSA obtains, uses, and retains foreign intelligence communications pursuant to section 702. Thus, we are to analyse whether existing privacy safeguards are built into the overall process, taking into consideration the loopholes present under section 702.

Section 702 of the amended version of FISA requires the government to develop targeting and minimization procedures that must later be approved by the FISC.[117] The FISC then publishes an opinion after the documents are submitted, elaborating on whether the updated and amended procedures meet the necessary standards. Generally, each agency, whether it is the NSA, FBI, or CIA, that receives information or data under section 702, has its own minimization procedures that must also be approved by the FISC. Our analysis will be based on the most recent opinion published by FISC on April 26, 2017,[118] approving the new amended minimization and

---

[117] Foreign Intelligence Surveillance Act. Title VII, Section 702 d e. 50. U.S.C. 1881a.

[118] FISC Memorandum and Opinion. Available at:

targeting procedures, which were filed by the Attorney General and Director of National Intelligence on March 30, 2017.[119] Finally, we are to summarize the FISC's findings and highlight those points that raise concern.

In relation to the targeting procedures, and as previously mentioned in this section, it appears that the revised procedures avoided concerns related to 'about' collection of information related to American persons. The targeting procedures generally govern how the executive branch determines that a targeted person believed to be outside the U.S. can lead to the acquisition of foreign intelligence information. When it comes to determining whether the acquisition targets non-U.S. persons outside the U.S., it appears that the document took into consideration various categories that could be considered reasonable enough to make such a determination. The three categories of information that the NSA analysts examine are; "the examination of the lead information the analysts have received regarding the potential target, research is conducted to

---

https://assets.documentcloud.org/documents/3718776/2016-Cert-FISC-Memo-Opin-Order-Apr-2017-1.pdf

[119] Documents available at: Minimization procedures:
https://assets.documentcloud.org/documents/3718777/2016-NSA-702-Minimization-Procedures-Mar-30-17.pdf
Targeting procedures: https://assets.documentcloud.org/documents/3718778/2016-NSA-702-Targeting-Procedures-Mar-30-17.pdf

determine whether the NSA knows the location of the person, and they seek to verify the target's location."[120] Hence, the NSA can be said to provide a critical assessment of how those three categories can be satisfied and met. The NSA further provided in its document that acquisitions conducted under these procedures will be limited to communications 'to' or 'from' persons targeted.[121] In addition, the NSA stresses that in its post-targeting analysis of a suspect, if the target is believed to have entered the United States, the NSA will first confirm such a conduct by targeting the suspect's telephone numbers or electronic communications. If it turns to be true, the NSA will immediately terminate the acquisition without delay.

Most importantly, and in relation to the protection of the privacy of American persons, the document explains that if the NSA determines that a target, who is initially believed to be a non-U.S. person is later suspected of being a U.S. person, certain procedures are to be followed. Such procedures include the termination of the acquisition without delay, determining whether a court order is necessary, and reporting the incident to the Department of Justice. Nevertheless the Attorney General

---

[120] Targeting procedures:
https://assets.documentcloud.org/documents/3718778/2016-NSA-702-Targeting-Procedures-Mar-30-17.pdf
[121] Ibid.

provides that in cases of utmost and immediate threat to national security, the NSA may depart from these procedures.

In relation to the minimization procedures, which take into consideration the acquisition, retention, use, and dissemination of any non-publicly available information related to American persons, there is a clear identification of who is to be considered a U.S. person when surveillance under section 702 is conducted.[122] NSA analysts will destroy communications of or concerning U.S. person without delay if the communication does not contain foreign intelligence information, or does not contain any evidence of a crime or any urgent matter. Hence, it falls upon NSA analysts to determine whether the information is domestic or foreign and whether it is relevant to the purpose of the acquisition. The document further provides that internet transactions, under the upstream program, that have been acquired after March 18, 2917 and are related to persons whom aren't supposed to be targeted in accordance with NSA's section 702, such as U.S. persons, and should therefore be destroyed the moment they are recognized. Hence, incidentally collected data relating to U.S. persons raises numerous issues, such as governmental officials using such data for a wide

---

[122] Minimization procedures:
https://assets.documentcloud.org/documents/3718777/2016-NSA-702-Minimization-Procedures-Mar-30-17.pdf

variety of purposes, which could be considered bulk collection due to the broad data collected. Nevertheless, the Attorney General's document provides equal playing ground to a certain extent as the document provides that communication involving U.S. persons may be retained or disseminated if it is believed to be relevant for future foreign intelligence surveillance.

Ultimately, although the 'about' collection of communication had been curtailed by the NSA, which means that the NSA will lose vital information, the FISC in its opinion still authorized the NSA to use American identifiers to query the newly captured internet communications under upstream for future intelligence investigations.[123] Thus, the full statuary logic is as follows; it is inevitable that there would be an acquisition of information relating to U.S. persons under surveillance, yet, such a conduct must be kept to a minimum, and in certain cases, such information ought to be destroyed.

Section 702 of may be overbroad as it may result in the collection, regardless of being incidental, of communications belonging to American persons without following legal protections. In reviewing the text of section 702, which is

---

[123] FISC Memorandum and Opinion. Available at:
https://assets.documentcloud.org/documents/3718776/2016-Cert-FISC-Memo-Opin-Order-Apr-2017-1.pdf

extensive, it may be perceived that it provides the public with transparency into the programs framework in relation to the collection of the data. Nevertheless, the extensiveness of section 702 does have an adverse effect, which is permitting the incidental collection of information and data belonging to American persons. Although the acquisition of such information may be legal due to being swept with other communications, the government here is using language loopholes in section 702, which is an overextension of national security measures. Also, such loopholes can be said to be tearing away the privacy protections of Americans who would simply like to connect with others abroad. Ultimately, the current rules may be inadequate in preventing the information gathered under section 702 for foreign intelligence purposes from being designated for domestic law enforcement.

With regards to minimization and targeting procedures, the NSA - after the newly enacted minimization and targeting procedures - appears to have taken strides towards better protecting American persons by setting out certain steps and categories that ought to be followed when conducting surveillance under section 702. Most importantly, although the collection of information belonging to U.S. persons has been curtailed to a large extent, it is still possible to acquire certain information under the flexible procedures established by the Attorney General and approved by the FISC.

Nevertheless, after the NSA has put an end to its 'about' collection earlier this year, what still places section 702 on a thin line is the fact that under the existing programs, the United States government may still be capable of 'incidentally' collecting a large scope of information and data belonging to American persons. Ultimately, with section 702 date of expiration approaching, we ought to expect heated debate around the scope of its surveillance programs till the 31st of December of this year. Yet, it ought to be stated that due to section 702 being the main authorization for the NSA to conduct foreign surveillance, it is unlikely that Congress will allow it to expire. Ultimately, the safeguards and protections contained in the minimization and targeting procedures under section 702 are reasonably designed to ensure a legitimate process when gathering foreign intelligence as well as ensuring an appropriate balance between the national security and privacy of American persons.

v.   Transparency of Government Surveillance Programs and the FISC

In response to the Snowden leaks, in August 2013, and after the passage of the USA Freedom Act, in 2015, the Office of the Director of National Intelligence (ODNI), under the direction of President Obama, created the 'IC on the Record' website which provides direct access to information related to the foreign surveillance activities of the United States government. This can be seen in section 215 of the USA PATRIOT Act and section 702 of FISA. The ODNI, through this website, published various documents and implementation plans related to section 215 and the operation of FISC. In addition, the website released, beginning in 2014, then in 2015, 2016 and 2017, statistics relating to the use of national security authorities, including the Foreign Intelligence Surveillance Act of 1978 and the USA PATRIOT Act of 2001. The most recent Annual Statistical Report, released in May 2017, revealed the breadth of surveillance by the NSA, and other intelligence agencies, where it was provided that under FISA Title V, the Business Records provision, and under section 215 of the USA PATRIOT Act, the NSA collected over 151 million phone call records from only forty-two targets.[124] In addition, the report estimated that under section 702 of FISA, there were 106,469 targets, in comparison to 94,386 in 2015, and 92,707 in 2014.[125]

---

[124] Statistical Transparency Report: Regarding The Use of National Security Authorities for Calendar Year 2016, IC on the record. Available at: https://icontherecord.tumblr.com/transparency/odni_transparencyreport_cy2016

It is important to consider that those statistics are after the USA Freedom Act ended the bulk collection of data and limited the query process, and after the NSA stated that it will halt its 'about' collection. Nevertheless, providing such statistical data is essential as it allows the public to know how many individuals have been caught-up in the NSA's surveillance programs.

Moreover, the Office of the Director of National Intelligence (ODNI) published the principles of Intelligence Transparency for the Intelligence Community in 2015 to "make appropriate and responsible transparency more coordinated, credible, understandable, and sustainable."[126] Those principles are intended to enhance the public understanding of the surveillance programs, whilst also protecting national security. When considering those principles, it can be seen that as to whether the NSA provides appropriate transparency to enhance public understanding and knowledge of the functions, roles, processes, and orders related to section 215 of the USA PATRIOT Act and section 702 of FISA, it is apparent that the

---

[125] Ibid

[126] Principles of Intelligence Transparency for the Intelligence Community, Office of the Director of National Intelligence. Available at:
https://www.dni.gov/index.php/ic-legal-reference-book/the-principles-of-intelligence-transparency-for-the-ic

intelligence community has taken steps to implement such a principle. Nevertheless, all the aforementioned steps taken in disclosing happenings under the Sections may have been purely the result of the Snowden revelations that pushed the government towards implementing certain principles and releasing vast amounts of data. Is this what it takes for the intelligence community to inform the public understanding of surveillance programs? Or were those disclosures merely made to cause minimal harm to national security.

Secrecy should be viewed as indispensable to the government's function as it protects the United States and its national security realm by controlling the information that could create an advantage over other nations. Similarly, openness, or transparency, also has its instrumental benefits, as it promotes more informed debate, permits public comprehension of governmental surveillance activities, and ultimately provides grounds on which public faith towards the government can flourish. Although criticisms still exist in intelligence transparency related to government surveillance programs, it is evident that the government has taken significant steps towards developing principles and criteria related to transparency within the intelligence community generally. Such increased transparency will enable the public to become more aware of what actually occurs within the FISC and how the NSA is conducting its surveillance. Ultimately, we must accept that governmental surveillance is inevitable, yet there must be a demand to make whatever occurs from investigations and Court opinions public within reason.

In relation to the FISC's transparency, and building upon the aftermath of the Snowden leaks, the FISC created its own website in June 2103 where it began publishing a docket after 35 years of being silent about governmental surveillance programs.[127] Through this website, the public is made capable of reading every pleading, filing, and opinion the Court has ever made. This public window contains documents related to FISC's operations, functions, and responses to inquiries. The website is under-progress, as opinions and filings are still in a scanned format, yet is still a significant step forward compared to prior years of non-disclosure.

Generally, the FISC has authority or the "jurisdiction to hear applications for and grant orders approving electronic surveillance anywhere within the United States." Prior to the passage of the USA Freedom Act, the FISC opinions were classified and there was no requirement for such opinions to be

---

[127] Available at: http://www.fisc.uscourts.gov/

made public. This made it difficult for the American people to fully evaluate the scope and impact of U.S. governmental surveillance programs. Nevertheless, with the passage of the USA Freedom Act in 2015, it was provided under section 402 that the FISC release novel interpretations of the law, which thus makes the FISC opinions part of common law, hence, legal authority for deciding subsequent cases. However, provisions under Title IV of the USA Freedom Act, 'Foreign Intelligence Surveillance Court Reforms,' are unclear as to whether or not there should be retroactive disclosure of FISC opinions prior to the passage of the USA Freedom Act. In quoting the ACLU in their case against FISC requiring that the Court releases classified decisions between 2001 and 2015, "These rulings are necessary to inform the public about the scope of the government's surveillance powers today." Thus, it ought to be reflected that having post September 11, 2001, FISC decisions released to the public will assist in establishing the legal basis upon which modern day governmental surveillance is being carried out.

Although the FISC's opinions may be held secret for national security purposes and due to the sensitivity of the intelligence community, the FISC's release of novel interpretations of the law will undoubtedly facilitate better public understanding of the development of the law. Hence, FISC decisions are being continuously declassified and released on the FISC's website and on the prior website, IC on the Record. Ultimately, the FISC's disclosure of any opinion the Court adopts is a step towards increased transparency.

Ultimately, and by reflecting the product of this chapter, it would be appropriate to quote Frank Church, the United States former Senator from Idaho (1957 - 1981), who chaired the investigative committee of the surveillance activities of the U.S. government in the mid-1970s when he warned that, "The NSA's capability at any time could be turned around on the American people, and no American would have any privacy left, such is the capability to monitor everything: telephone conversations, telegrams, it doesn't matter."

2. Government Surveillance Programs in Great Britain

Similar to the United States, Great Britain has agencies responsible for collecting and producing foreign and domestic intelligence. The main British intelligence agencies - The Security Service (MI5), the Secret Intelligence Service (MI6), and the Government Communications Headquarters (GCHQ) -

all contribute through their intelligence assessments to the general conduct of the United Kingdom's foreign relations, and thus maintaining the nation's national security.

The Security Service (MI5) is responsible for domestic intelligence and security, in which the agency performs counter terrorism and counter espionage intelligence gathering and analysis. Thus, MI5 could be compared to the FBI in the United States. As MI5's focus is that of domestic intelligence, their role is defined under the Security Service Act of 1989, "the protection of national security and in particular its protection against threats such as terrorism, espionage and sabotage, the activities of agents of foreign powers..."[128]

In relation to its intelligence activities, it has been reported that after the September 11, 2001, attacks in the United States, MI5 started collecting data in bulk within the United Kingdom under section 94 of the Telecommunications Act of 1984,[129] which permits the bulk collection of data using powers which are exercised without any oversight. Hence, this was reported to be for national security interests. Thus, instead of adopting the Regulation of Investigatory Powers Act of 2000,[130] which

---

[128] Security Service Act 1989. Chapter 5. 1 (2).

[129] Telecommunications Act of 1984. Article 94.

[130] The Regulation of Investigatory Powers Act of 2000.

grants and regulates the powers of public bodies to carry out surveillance and investigation, the government chose a Bill that lacked oversight and Parliamentary scrutiny in general. As expected, there was a public backlash to the MI5 spying on UK persons after the Home Secretary at the time, Theresa May, announced it to the public in November 2015; this came as PM May revealed the intelligence measures in the draft of the 'Investigatory Powers Act' that was enacted later on in 2016.[131]

The Secret Intelligence Service (MI6) is responsible for foreign intelligence gathering and analysis. Thus, MI6 can be considered the equivalent of the CIA in the United States. MI6's core mission is the protection of the United Kingdom's national security and navigating any risks the nation may face. MI6's functions are placed under the statuary footing of the Intelligence Services Act of 1994, where its role is described as being, "to obtain and provide information relating to the actions or intentions of persons outside the British Islands; and to perform other tasks relating to the actions or intentions of such persons."[132]

---

[131] Tom Whitehead, MI5 and GCHQ secretly bulk collecting British public's phone and email records for years, Theresa May reveals, The Telegraph (No 4, 2015), http://www.telegraph.co.uk/news/uknews/terrorism-in-the-uk/11976008/MI5-and-GCHQ-secretly-bulk-collecting-British-publics-phone-and-email-records-for-years-Theresa-May-reveals.html
[132] Intelligence Services Act of 1994. Chapter 13. 1 (1)(a)(b).

Finally, the Government Communications Headquarters (GCHQ) are responsible for gathering and analysing signals intelligence (SIGINT) in which they intercept communications and data. Thus, GCHQ can be considered the equivalent of the NSA in the United States. Similar to MI6, the GCHG is also given statuary basis under the Intelligence Services Act of 1994, where its role is stated as, "in the interests of national security, with particular reference to the defence and foreign policies of Her Majesty's government in the United Kingdom; or in the interests of the economic wellbeing of the UK; or in the support of the prevention or detection of serious crime."[133]

GCHQ has certainly received wide media attention since the Snowden disclosures in 2013 of GCHQ's activities and its cooperation with the United States NSA.[134] As previously mentioned in the introduction of this book, Snowden revealed that GCHQ uses a computer system, named Tempora, to buffer internet communications via social media that are extracted from fibre-optic cables. After gaining access to such communications, the GCHQ stores the data in large amounts

---

[133] Intelligence Services Act of 1994. Chapter 13. 3 (2)(a)(b)(c).
[134] Kadhim Shubber, A simple guide to GCHQ's internet surveillance programme Tempora, WIRED (June 24, 2013), http://www.wired.co.uk/article/gchq-tempora-101

without having a specific target in order to process and search the data in the long run. In his revelations, Snowden provided that the data collected under the Tempora program was later shared with the NSA. Thus, those revelations about the ability of both agencies to snoop on the private data of people certainly was not well-received.

In addition, it ought to be reflected that Tempora may be more stringent than the NSA's PRISM program, for one main reason, which is that Tempora does not only take in the metadata of communications like PRISM, but it takes both the content and associated metadata. Tempora takes in more, both in scope and scale. Thus, Tempora does not only infringe upon the privacy rights of UK citizens, but also that of other nations, including U.S. citizens.

In relation to the legal justifications to Tempora. It appears that the GCHQ used Chapter 1 of the Regulation of Investigatory Powers Act of 2000 to justify its bulk collection of data providing that the acquisition of the communications was performed externally, hence, the communications can be read or listened to indiscriminately.[135] In addition, seeing as the

---

[135] Owen Bowcott and James Ball, Social Media mass surveillance is permitted by law, says top UK official, The Guardian (June 12, 2014), https://www.theguardian.com/world/2014/jun/17/mass-surveillance-social-media-

servers of the social media corporations, such as Facebook, are based in the United States, the communications are considered 'external' unlike the internal that require a warrant to be looked into.[136] Ultimately, and under this program, it seems that the GCHQ is using a weak legal justification to sidestep the need to protect privacy rights of individuals and feel that they have the opportunity to indiscriminately collect and monitor the social media of private individuals. Quoting Eric King, Previous Deputy Director of Privacy International, "The safeguards provided by RIPA pertaining to the interception of 'internal' communications do not in fact result in any meaningful protections for such communications privacy when applied to the modern communications system."[137]

As the aforementioned actions by the intelligence agencies in the past have been dependent on laws that have been drafted prior to the Internet era or may be simply flimsy, it is reflected that the law that existed was complicated and ambiguous as it was buried in different Acts. Building up to the

permitted-uk-law-charles-farr
[136] The Regulation of Investigatory Powers Act of 2000. Chapter 1. Section 8 (1) and Section 8 (4)
[137] Owen Bowcott and James Ball, Social Media mass surveillance is permitted by law, says top UK official, The Guardian (June 12, 2014), https://www.theguardian.com/world/2014/jun/17/mass-surveillance-social-media-permitted-uk-law-charles-farr

newly enacted 'Investigatory Powers Act 2016', the below paragraphs will elaborate on how the 2016 Bill does not make things better for privacy advocates, as it marks a scarier shift due to its controversy and offering of unprecedented new powers relating to the bulk collection requirement that in turn is invasive towards privacy rights.

The Investigatory Powers Act of 2016, also known as the Snoopers Charter by privacy campaigners,[138] was passed by the United Kingdom Government on December 30, 2016.[139] It ought to be stated in the outset that this law is the most expansive surveillance law in the West, even more so than those in the United States that have faced extensive scrutiny. This Act replaced large sections of the Regulation of Investigatory Powers Act of 2000, and replaced the Data Retention and Investigatory Powers Act of 2014. Generally, the Act authorizes activities that were already taking place, but not properly outlined, such as the bulk collection of data, interception of communications, and retention requirements on communication providers.

---

[138] Such as; Liberty: Protecting Civil Liberties Promoting Human Rights. Available at: https://liberty.e-activist.com/ea-action/action?ea.client.id=1826&ea.campaign.id=44061 & https://www.liberty-human-rights.org.uk/campaigning/people-vs-snoopers-charter
[139] Investigatory Powers Act 2016. Chapter 25.

Despite heavy lobbying by privacy activists and tech corporations prior to the official enactment of this Act, its eventual passing was justified under the basis that it was necessary for the protection of national security. Additionally, due to the expiration date of the Data Retention and Investigatory Powers Act of 2014 approaching, the government was under pressure to finalize the Investigatory Powers Act of 2016.

Furthermore, this Act, as will be discussed, has a broad scope that flows from the heart of the Act, where it defines a telecommunications operator as to include both private and public networks and service providers.[140] Hence, not just carriers, but also online storage providers, which operate from the United Kingdom or are originally in the United Kingdom. Below we are to outline the main sections that have given rise to controversy and outrage by privacy proponents and tech corporations, and why Snowden considered this as "the most extreme surveillance in the history of western democracy."[141]

---

[140] Investigatory Powers Act 2016. Article 261 (10)

[141] Nadia Prupis, UK set to approve most extreme spy bill in history of western democracy, Common Dreams (Nov 18, 2016), https://www.commondreams.org/news/2016/11/18/uk-set-approve-most-extreme-spy-bill-history-western-democracy

The main parts of the discussion include the retention of data by communication service providers, the bulk interception of communications, and the bulk acquisition of communications data.

In relation to the retention of communications data,[142] the Investigatory Powers Act provides that the Secretary of State may require, via a retention notice, a telecommunication operator to retain relevant communications data for a period not longer than twelve months.[143] In addition, the Act provides a wide scope for the Secretary of State to include in the retention notice, as the notice may relate to different purposes, the periods for which the data is to be retained, or could even relate to the retention of all data.[144] In addition, this section, or the Act in general, places a requirement on communication providers to collect and retain communications data, thus allowing law enforcement agencies to snoop through the personal life of individuals. It is vital to elaborate on how the Act defined 'communication'; as the definition is so broad that it does not only cover person to person, but also person to

---

[142] Such data refers to records of internet services that have been accessed by a device.

[143] Investigatory Powers Act 2016. Article 87 (1)(3)

[144] Investigatory Powers Act 2016. Article 87 (2)

machine, and machine to machine communications.[145] Hence, those are all grouped into this legislation.

Nevertheless, section 87 also provides safeguards for the retention of data by communication providers, for instance, it does not necessarily mean that an obligation will be imposed on communications providers, as no provider has an obligation to retain, disclose data, or assist with interception of data unless or until the provider is actually served with a notice or warrant by the Secretary of State or some public authority. In addition, it is required that the Secretary of State must consider that the retention notice is necessary and proportionate in light of what is set under section 61 (7) of the Act.[146] Nevertheless, the grounds set under section 61 (7) are so broad and surreal that they are not merely limited to the protection of national security, as stated by UK spokesmen. Hence, purposes where obtaining communications data is permitted include, preventing disorder, national security, protecting public health, mitigating damage to physical or mental health, or exercising functions related to the regulation of financial matters.[147]

---

[145] Investigatory Powers Act 2016. Article 261 (2)(b)
[146] Investigatory Powers Act 2016. Article 87 (1)
[147] Investigatory Powers Act 2016. Article 61 (7) (a, b, c, d, e, f, g, h, I, j)

In relation to the bulk powers under the Act, the Act gives permission for the Bulk interception of data and the bulk acquisition of data. Although it is indeed a vital tool in obtaining foreign intelligence and identifying individuals and organisations overseas that have the capability of posing a threat to the United Kingdom, nevertheless, collecting, intercepting, or hacking of communications in bulk is an infringement on privacy rights, regardless of whether the targets are from the United Kingdom or not. When it comes to the bulk interception of communications, the Act provides that bulk interception warrants should be provided under two conditions. Firstly, that the purpose of the interception of overseas-related communication or / and the obtainment of secondary data which comprises almost all sorts of data and enables the identification of senders and recipients.[148] The second condition is that the warrant limits the person to whom the warrant is addressed to secure the interception while being transmitted, obtaining secondary data from communications transmitted, or / and the disclosure of anything obtained under the warrant.[149] When it comes to the Bulk acquisition of data, the Act provides that the Secretary of State may issue a warrant related to bulk acquisition as long as it is necessary for national

---

[148] Investigatory Powers Act 2016. Article 136 (2) (3). Article 137 (3) (4) (5)
[149] Investigatory Powers Act 2016. Section 136 (4)

security, preventing or detecting crime, or the economic well-being of the United Kingdom. Hence, this must all fall back to the protection of national security.[150]

Nevertheless, and regardless of the safeguards that have been presented by the Act following all the conducts carried out in bulk, such as the requirement that national security must always be a statutory purpose when a warrant is sought to collect material in bulk. Allowing the British intelligence agencies to collect and intercept communications in bulk of persons outside the UK will permit the filtering of material in order to identify communications of intelligence value. Activities conducted in bulk will be limited to intelligence agencies and only for limited purposes to protect the nation, the data will be shared with limited personnel, having codes of practice in place, or even the requirement that warrants must contain a consideration of necessity and proportionality are all clearly unnecessary and disproportionate as will be discussed below.

Therefore, as long as the form of the collection, acquisition, or interception of data is carried out in bulk, personal information or data relating to both UK persons and citizens from other

---

[150] Investigatory Powers Act 2016. Section 158 (1) (2)

nations will be infringed upon. Part 6 of the Act, which is concerned with the Bulk Powers places mass surveillance powers, as well as additional and clearer bulk surveillance methods on a statuary footing. The United States of America abandoned its bulk collection under section 215 of the USA PATRIOT Act following the Snowden revelation, yet the United Kingdom introduced a Bill that protects such unnecessary activities that threat privacy rights and civil liberties. The United Kingdom has not produced one unique or critical contribution of the bulk collection of data in combating terrorism and thus protecting national security. Also, the Act does not just infringe on the privacy of UK persons, as it legalises what the GCHQ has been doing for years, under Tempora, including 'snooping' on all data that passes through fibre-optic cables.

In support of the 2016 Surveillance Bill, Theresa May, stated that the Bill is essential to keeping the UK secure as well as serving in underpinning the duties and conducts of intelligence agencies and law enforcement in the years to come.[151] May, through her continuous statements in support of the Bill, reflected that such a law would be a modern fit as it has the

---

[151] Matt Burges, UN privacy chief: UK surveillance bill is 'worse than scary', WIRED (Nov 10, 2015), http://www.wired.co.uk/article/surveillance-investigatory-powers-scary-joseph-cannataci

capability, in light of technological advancements, of responding to emerging threats. Nevertheless, with existing EU law and prospective GDPR, did Theresa May and parties in support of the Bill take the co-existence of both bills into consideration? In staying relevant to current or upcoming events, we are to mainly base the discussion here on the conflict that may arise between the current UK 2016 Bill, existing EU law, and upcoming EU law, the General Data Protection Regulation, which is expected to be implemented across the EU by May 2018.

In summary, the GDPR is the most comprehensive document that enhances digital privacy of persons and individual rights Europe has seen so far. The GDPR applies to "any information relating to an identified or identifiable natural person," thus, it applies to natural persons and applies to any agency or body that processes personal data within territorial limits. What should be taken into consideration here is the section under the Investigatory Powers Act that requires communication service providers to collect and retain internet communication records for a year. Yet, under this Act, corporations are not required to inform persons that their data will be stored and consent is absent. Under the proposed GDPR draft, Individuals have a right to be informed and a right to have their data erased - the right to be forgotten.   Therefore, as companies are required to acquire informed consent from their customers' typically through a privacy notice with total transparency on how the data is to be implemented, as well as whether the data is to be acquired by a third party, such as the UK government in our case. In relation to the right to be forgotten, which is a right endowed to EU citizens by the GDOR, it may be challenging for UK persons to request the deletion or removal of their data, as it is not an absolute right. Nonetheless, the data could be erased if persons object to the way their data will be processed and withdraw their consent.

In relation to the aforementioned section related to the retention of data under the Investigatory Powers Act of 2016, the EU Court of Justice ruling in the Digital Rights Ireland case in April 2014,[152] and the Court's ruling in Joined cases Tele2 and Watson in 2016 [153] raise the question of how the 2016 UK Bill will manage to co-exist with the EU. In 2014, Digital Rights Ireland, a digital rights advocacy group, challenged the EU Data Retention Directive which "obliged EU member states to

---

[152] Digital Rights Ireland v Minister for Communications, minister for Justice, Commissioner of the Garda Síochána, Ireland and the Attorney General (C-293/12)

[153] Tele 2, Sverige AB v Post-och Telestyrelsen and Secretary of State for the Home Department v. Watson, Brice, and Lewis (Joined Cases C-203/15 & C-698/15)

require communications service providers to retain communications data for between 6 and 24 months."[154] The CJEU in this case declared the Directive invalid for violating fundamental human rights. This ruling was based on the fact that the Directive led to disproportionate interference with the rights contained in Articles 7 and 8 of the EU Charter of Fundamental Rights.[155] Those Articles relate to the fundamental right to respect of private life and to the protection of personal data. Although advocates in this case argue that retention rules are vital for agencies and law authorities to investigate and combat crime and terrorism, but the Court ruled that bulk data retention endangers individuals' right to privacy. In addition, the Court further provided in its judgment that the retained data will allow for very precise conclusions concerning private lives, everyday habits, and social environments frequented. Thus, the Court reflects that the fact that the data retained will be used without the subscriber being

---

[154] Data Retention Directive (2006/24/EC)

[155] EU Charter of Fundamental Rights. Article 7 "Respect for Private and Family Life: Everyone has the right to respect for his or her private and family life, home and communications."
Article 8 "Protection of Personal Data: 1. Everyone has the right to the protection of personal data concerning him or her. 2. Such data must be processed fairly for specified purposes and on the basis of the consent of the person concerned or some other legitimate basis laid down by law. Everyone has the right of access to data which has been collected concerning him or her, and the right to have it rectified. 3. Compliance with these rules shall be subject to control by an independent authority."

informed is likely to generate the feeling that personal lives are under constant surveillance.

Furthermore, in December 2016, the Court of Justice of the European Union, in clarifying the impact of the Digital Rights Ireland case on EU Member States national data retention legislation, ruled that EU Member States cannot pass laws that require communications service providers to carry out indiscriminate retention of communications data. This was a ruling in joined cases, Home Office v. Watson & Tele2 Sverige. Those cases concerned appropriateness from a human rights perspective of national legislation relating to data retention even after the Court had struck down the 2006 EU Data Retention Directive in the Digital Rights Ireland case in 2014.

The Swedish case resulted from a dispute between the Swedish Post and Telecom Authority and the Swedish service providers who resisted a data retention order, while the British case was brought by British Members of Parliament against the Data Retention and Investigatory Powers Act of 2014 that was enacted to provide legal basis for the retention of data after domestic legislation fell as a consequence to the CJEU invalidating the 2006 Directive in the Digital Rights Ireland case in 2014. Both judgements were set under the context of the Privacy and Electronic Communications Directive.[156] This Directive requires the protection of privacy and confidentiality in the electronic communications sector

As an overview of the British (Watson) case, which is of utmost relevance to this discussion, as it was raised by British petitioners challenging the Data Retention and Investigatory Powers Act of 2014, which expired on December 31, 2016, and was replaced by the Investigatory Powers Act 2016 on January 1, 2017. This Act allowed the UK's intelligence agencies to access internet and phone records of individuals, and was deemed invalid after the CJEU struck down the 2006 EU Data Retention Directive. In its ruling, the CJEU provided that the reading of the ePrivacy Directive should consider the European Charter of Fundamental Rights, and that provisions related to indiscriminate retention of data exceed the limits of what can be considered necessary and such retention cannot be justified within a democratic society. Furthermore, the CJEU claims that data retention legislation, such as the expired 2014 UK Bill, is inconsistent with EU law in which the national legislation allows agencies and law enforcement access to retained data for

---

[156] Privacy and Electronic Communications Directive (Directive 2002/58/EC). Also known as the ePrivacy Directive.

purposes of fighting general crimes rather than serious crimes. There is a provision in the legislation that allows general and indiscriminate retention of data of all users and subscribers to communications providers. Although the CJEU does not specifically indicate what states should consider as 'strictly necessary' when it comes to retaining the data, but it provides within the aforementioned 2016 joined ruling that "data retention legislation must "indicate in what circumstances and under which conditions a data retention measure may, as a preventive measure, be adopted, thereby ensuring that such a measure is limited to what is strictly necessary."[157] Nevertheless, it ought to be reflected that European judgments resulting from appeal cases do not have an effect in the United Kingdom until observed by a British judge. Hence, a domestic British Court will ultimately decide the interpretation of the CJEU rulings.

Considering that the Investigatory Powers Act 2016 is an extension to the expired 2014 Bill, it is not compliant with any of the CJEU's judgments as the 2016 Bill allows access to retained data by a number of government bodies, and it requires communications providers to conduct general and

---

[157] Tele 2, Sverige AB v Post-och Telestyrelsen and Secretary of State for the Home Department v. Watson, Brice, and Lewis (Joined Cases C-203/15 & C-698/15)

indiscriminate retention of data. Furthermore, the CJEU does not prevent states from adopting legislation that permits the targeted retention of data for the purpose of combating serious crime, such as terrorism. According to the CJEU's ruling, paragraph 90 "a state may only mandate data retention in order to safeguard national security - that is, State security - defence, public security, and the prevention, investigation, detection and prosecution of criminal offences or of unauthorised use of the electronic communication system."[158] Nevertheless, the 2016 UK Bill provides for indiscriminate and general retention of all traffic data of users as well as the grounds for retaining data under section 61 (7) are so broad that they are not strictly limited to terrorism or other serious crimes, but permit retention for public disorder, financial matters, etc. Ultimately, the ruling in the Watson case casts doubt over the legality of the Investigatory Powers Act 2016 which clearly extends the bulk retention of data powers contained in its predecessor, the Data Retention and Investigatory Powers Act 2014.

Hence, it can be said that government mandated data retention, such as that contained under the UK 2016 Bill, impacts a significant number of ordinary users as it compromises online anonymity, the right to free expression, and most importantly

___

[158] Ibid.

the right to privacy. As the 2016 UK Bill obliges, through a warrant, communication service providers to acquire and store the activity of customers regardless of whether or not they are suspected of a crime, it is doubtful that it will survive current and upcoming EU law. Thus, the Court's rulings reflect that general and indiscriminate data retention violates EU fundamental human rights and is thus unlawful. Ultimately, legal challenges against the Investigatory Powers Act of 2016 are seemingly inevitable and having such a law in place could cause a stand-off situation. The aforementioned case law does not only demonstrate that the EU Data Retention Directive is unlawful, but also that all EU Member States that have the same data retention requirements are unlawful.

As discussed, the provisions of the Investigatory Powers Act 2016 are controversial, yet, it is vital to examine the reasons behind the British government's current controls, and why the government feels that such measures and powers do protect the privacy of individuals. In relation to the transparency of the Investigatory Powers Act of 2016, the Bill holds the intelligence agencies accountable to the Information Commissioner, who in turn must monitor compliance with the restrictions or requirements set under the Bill, which are related to the safeguarding, retention, and destruction of data.[159] The

Information Commissioners also have great audit powers as they must keep under review the functions relating to the interception of communications, the acquisitions and retention of data, and interference with equipment.[160] Furthermore, the Bill provides safeguards by including the requirement of obtaining judicial approval prior to warrants being enforced. A Judicial Commissioner is obliged to review whether the warrant is necessary on relevant grounds, such as purposes relevant to national security, preventing serious crime, or even in the interests of economic well-being.[161] Although the Secretary of State retains the responsibility of granting warrants, but a Judicial Commissioner will ensure, under this Bill, that a warrant is lawful.[162] The Bill also provides that the Judicial Commissioners must apply the same principles that would be applied by an ordinary court for applications related to judicial review. Such oversight thus provides a certain level of reassurance over the functions of intelligence agencies. The oversight arrangements are set under Part 8 of the Bill.

The aforementioned parts of the Bill, such as the bulk collection of data, the retention of communications data, and

---

[159] Investigatory Powers Act 2016. Section 244.

[160] Investigatory Powers Act 2016. Section 229

[161] Investigatory Powers Act 2016. Section 23

[162] Investigatory Powers Act 2016. Section 19

the bulk interception of data, have all existed or have been carried out previously by the British government, where they were justified under previous Bills, such as the Data Retention and Investigatory Powers Act and the Telecommunications Act. The new 2016 Bill simply brought such powers previously and currently exercised to light. Ultimately, the 2016 Bill increased transparency around the powers that the British agencies have exercised throughout the years, such as the interception and retention of communications data; hence, the Bill does achieve the goal of increasing transparency when it comes to obtaining internet and phone communications data.

With regards to the backlash the Bill has gotten since its enactment, Liberty, a human rights campaign organization, launched a legal challenge against the Investigatory Powers Act in March of 2017.[163] The group raised approximately £50,000 towards legal fees that would finance the legal action they intend to take.[164] The basis for their action was to challenge the lawfulness of the following powers; the Bulk hacking in which the policies and agencies are permitted to access, control and alter electronic devices such as computers and tablets on an

---

[163] Clare Hopping, Liberty launches legal challenge against Investigatory Powers Act, ITPRO (Mar 2, 2017), http://www.itpro.co.uk/it-legislation/28251/liberty-launches-legal-challenge-against-investigatory-powers-act
[164] Ibid.

industrial scale regardless of whether the owners are suspects in a crime. Another issue was the bulk interception of data in which the government was allowed to read online messages, texts, and emails, without any suspicion of wrongdoing. In addition, the bulk acquisition of communications data and internet history was a basis for the suit in which service providers and communication corporations were forced to hand over records of the public's phone calls, emails, texts, and internet history to state agencies. Hence, agencies could store, profile, and data mine at their will. Nevertheless, GCHQ personnel, such as David Wells, a former intelligence officer at GCHQ, stated that the bulk collection of data have allowed intelligence analysts to ask smarter questions, and that it has a unique value in comparison to other intelligence approaches.[165]

Ultimately, although the Investigatory Powers Act was intended to be a law that would replace existing UK broken laws, yet, instead of restricting mass surveillance, it put all the powers into one law. Thus, the Investigatory Powers Act is inadequate in protecting the population from intrusions into their privacy due to mass surveillance. Hence, Amber Rudd's,

---

[165] David Wells, Investigatory Powers Bill - the case for mass surveillance, ComputerWeekly.com. available at:
http://www.computerweekly.com/opinion/Investigatory-Powers-Bill-the-case-for-mass-surveillance

Home Secretary, statement that "The Investigatory Powers Act is world-leading legislation that provides unprecedented transparency and substantial privacy protection." stands on very weak grounds.[166] Yes, Theresa May's statements and constant pushing for harsher surveillance laws prior to her becoming Prime Minister may have been on the legitimate grounds to combat terrorism and protect the United Kingdom's national security, "It is their license to operate -- with the democratic approval of Parliament -- to protect our national security and the public's safety."[167] Nevertheless, was May aware that this Act endangers the privacy rights of British individuals? Ultimately, this is a precarious precedent to set and many of the provisions do require extensive testing and reconsideration as they undermine the privacy rights of individuals.

3. The Privacy Dilemma

"In a digital era, privacy must be a priority. Is it just me, or is secret blanket surveillance obscenely outrageous?"[168]

---

[166] GOV.UK, Investigatory Powers Bill receives Royal Assent, (Nov 29, 2016), https://www.gov.uk/government/news/investigatory-powers-bill-receives-royal-assent

[167] Katie Collins, UK surveillance law marks a 'worse than scary' shift, C Net (No 29, 2016), https://www.cnet.com/news/snoopers-charter-investigatory-powers-bill-royal-assent-surveillance-uk/

Al Gore

45th Vice President of the United States

As portrayed in the first and second chapter, surveillance programs in both the United States and the United Kingdom are raising concerns with regards to safeguarding privacy. Yet, as will be portrayed in this section is that governmental surveillance programs in the United States face more scrutiny and thus safeguard privacy more than programs in the United Kingdom. Regardless of whether this could be attributed to the Snowden revelations or not, the United States has established review groups and specialized courts to oversee such programs. On the other hand, the United Kingdom took an opposite direction after the Snowden revelations, where the government passed the Investigatory Powers Act in 2016 which gave the intelligence community more powers to infringe upon privacy, such as the mass collection of data. In this section we are to look at whether surveillance programs - or surveillance in general - within both nations incorporates the privacy protections provided by the federal and constitutional laws,

---

[168] Suzanne Goldenberg, Al Gore: NSA's secret surveillance program 'not really the American way', The Guardian (June 14, 2013),
https://www.theguardian.com/world/2013/jun/14/al-gore-nsa-surveillance-unamerican

when it comes to the United States, and by the parliamentary laws related to the United Kingdom.

In relation to the United States Surveillance programs - E.O. 12333, Section 215 of the USA PATRIOT Act, and Section 702 of FISA -, which may not be similar in terms of functionality and role, yet they have all made significant strides in recent years when it comes to safeguarding the privacy of both U.S. persons and non--U.S. persons. For instance, the passage of the USA Freedom Act changed the entire scope and role of section 215 as it ended the bulk collection of data by the NSA and the FBI. This Act allowed for data to be retained by communications service providers, and the query process became two hops instead of three. In relation to section 702 of FISA, the USA Freedom Act may not have introduced any significant changes, yet the NSA, after being subjected to criticism by the FISC due to its about collection which enabled the agency to collect content data, announced earlier this year - April 26, 2017 - that it will be discontinuing its about collection, which has been praised as a positive reaction in the right direction. Yes, criticisms still exist, for the possibility of incidentally collecting information or data relating to American persons under section 702 - backdoor searches – remains. Nevertheless, the situation has improved greatly since

September 11, 2011, or even since the FISA Amendments Act of 2008.

The Fourth Amendment to the United States Constitution was added to the Bill of Rights in order to protect people from having their homes and private properties searched without a proper warrant. It specifically states, *"The right of the people to be secure in their persons, houses, papers, and effects, against unreasonable searches and seizures, shall not be violated, and no Warrants shall issue, but upon probable cause, supported by Oath or affirmation, and particularly describing the place to be searched, and the persons or things to be seized."* [169] Relating this constitutional right to NSA surveillance raises the issue of whether the NSA has violated the Fourth Amendment to the United States Constitution. This includes the collection of data and the prohibition on unreasonable searches, whether the intelligence community has probable cause to carry out surveillance, and whether persons have a reasonable expectation of privacy. Generally, due to technological advancements, the government now possess capabilities to collect, store, and analyse data that were not available when such cases - as portrayed below - were decided.

---

[169] Fourth Amendment to the United States Constitution.

There have been cases relating to governmental surveillance, dating back to 1928. For instance, the court in *Olmstead v United States* declined to extend Fourth Amendment protection to government wiretapping of telephone conversations, and held that as the case involved phone conversations, not physical artefacts; there was no Fourth Amendment violation.[170] Nevertheless, the opinion by Justice Brandeis certainly defines how such cases are now ruled when he stated, "The evil incident to invasion of the privacy of the telephone is far greater than that involved in tampering with the mails. Whenever a telephone line is tapped, the privacy of the persons at both ends of the line is invaded...". To briefly outline another case, which may be the most significant, in *Katz v. United States*, the court overturned the Olmstead decision as it held that the Fourth Amendment does protect non-tangible things such as phone calls and electronic transmissions.[171] The court in Katz further provided that the Fourth Amendment protects persons and not places from unreasonable intrusion, and that even in public places, one may have a reasonable expectation of privacy in his person. Ultimately, the court - J. Harlan - in this case set a two-part test for the Fourth Amendment to provide protection for individuals and not to certain places.

---

[170] 277 U.S. 438 (1928)

[171] 389 U.S. 347 (1967)

First, the person must have exhibited an actual expectation of privacy (subjective test), and, second, the expectation must be reasonable (objective test). Those are interesting cases as they demonstrate the Supreme Court's belief that in certain situations a bright line rule will not cover every situation.

What is of utmost relevance to this discussion is the Supreme Court established rule, the 'Third-party Doctrine.' The 1976 case of *United States v. Miller*, and the 1979 case of *Smith v. Maryland*, the 'Third-party' doctrine found its initial stance. In *Smith v. Maryland*, the Supreme Court ruled that persons who voluntarily give information or data to third parties, such as internet or communications service providers, have no reasonable expectation of privacy.[172] This ruling followed from the *Miller* case where the Supreme Court held that, "the Fourth Amendment does not prohibit the obtaining of information revealed to a third party and conveyed by him [depositor] to Government authorities, even if the information is revealed on the assumption that it will be used only for a limited purpose and the confidence placed in the third party will not be betrayed."[173] Thus, both cases solidified what is currently known as the third-party doctrine.

---

[172] 422 U.S. 735 (1979)

[173] 425 U.S. 435 (1976)

Furthermore, as can be concluded from the text of the Fourth Amendment, only when a conduct constitutes a search or a seizure could Fourth Amendment restrictions be applied. Seeing as the NSA does not obtain those internet or communications information or data directly from American persons under its programs; under section 215 of the USA PATRIOT Act, the data is to be held by private telecommunication providers, and the NSA can only obtain data about targeted individuals after obtaining permission from the FISC. However, although under section 702 of FISA, the NSA collects internet communications from internet companies under PRISM, the Supreme Court till this day has not made a determination on the stance of 'internet' communications being collected by the government. Nevertheless, under *United States v. Warshak*, the court stated that, "given the fundamental similarities between email and traditional forms of communication, it would defy common sense to afford emails lesser Fourth Amendment protection."[174] However, there is still no express rule on this issue by the Supreme Court. Thus, as service providers disclose such personal records to the NSA, the NSA could argue that such conduct does not qualify as a search under the Fourth Amendment, seeing as United States

---

[174] 631 F.3d 266 (6th Cir, 2010)

persons voluntarily disclose personal information to those service providers. Furthermore, the government could further argue that NSA surveillance programs are not significantly broader than the precedents set in both *Maryland* and *Miller*, due to the amendments introduced by the USA Freedom Act to section 215,[175] and the NSA halting its 'about' collection which dramatically decreases and perhaps eliminates data of U.S. persons collected. Under both programs, United States persons cannot be targeted directly, as under section 215 it depends on whether the person has terrorist ties and under section 702 it depends on scattered or incidentally collected information under the 'about' collection or under MCT. Not to forget to mention that those foreign persons targeted under the NSA programs lack any Fourth Amendment protections.

Nevertheless, the third-party doctrine has faced criticism as well as urges to rethink its foundation within the legal community, for instance, in the 2012 case of *United States v. Jones*, where the Supreme Court ruled that "the installation of a GPS tracking device on Jones' vehicle, without a warrant, constituted an unlawful search under the Fourth Amendment." Although this case dealt with a different question unrelated to

---

[175] Ending the bulk collection of data, data to be retained by communications providers, and the two hop query process.

the third-part doctrine, Associate Justice Sotomayor used her concurrence to reflect her dissatisfaction with the doctrine where she provided that, "it may be necessary to reconsider the premise that an individual has no reasonable expectation of privacy in information voluntarily disclosed to third parties. This approach is ill suited to the digital age, in which people reveal a great deal of information about themselves to third parties in the course of carrying out mundane tasks..."[176] Nevertheless, her statements are merely an opinion and have not been tested.

It is currently an open question on whether the United States Supreme Court will scrutinize the NSA's surveillance programs and apply old legal concepts to 21st-century communications technology, in addition to whether such programs - PRIMS, Upstream, or section 215 - comply with Fourth Amendment privacy rights. Also, predicting where the Supreme Court will take Fourth Amendment protections in connection with advanced technological uses is based on opinions and vague suggestions set forth in 'ancient' cases is precarious. Hence, the Katz case does not dictate what a reasonable expectation of privacy is, or what should be the result, but it is intended to provide a neutral framework that could be used in evaluating

---

[176] 132 S. Ct. 949 (2012)

both sides of the argument. Also, it solely falls upon the Supreme Court to actually change the third-party doctrine. Therefore, if the Justices wish to conclude that the NSA surveillance programs are unconstitutional, they must provide a reason for why they believe the programs should fall outside the scope of the third-party doctrine. Ultimately, and from a personal perspective, if one is unaware of the full capabilities of the United States government, then such persons do not have a right to expect privacy. Also, the NSA surveillance program's role in gathering foreign intelligence is vital in preventing terrorism within the United States. Thus, with the absence of individual warrants, and with the presence of adequate minimization procedures, targeting procedures, and oversight by the FISC - especially under section 702 programs - privacy advocates must take into consideration that such governmental intrusion, even if incidental, is reasonable for the protection of the nation and its persons.

In relation to whether the British Government respects and safeguards the privacy of its persons when conducting government surveillance, the Human Rights Act of 1998 comes into play. Generally, the human rights contained within the Human Rights Act of 1998 are based on the articles of the European Convention on Human Rights (ECHR). This Act protects a wide variety of rights, such as the right to life, prohibition of torture, protection and slavery and forced labour, the right to education, and most importantly, the right to privacy. Article 8 of the Human Rights Act protects the right to have respect for privacy, where it specifically protects against unnecessary surveillance or intrusion into a person's life.[177] Nevertheless, section 2 of Article 8 specifically provides that the public authority has the right to interfere with the right to privacy when national security or public safety is at stake.[178] Hence, while the right to privacy encompasses a wide array of situations, yet it is lawfully limited under the Act.

The United Kingdom recently introduced - as previously mentioned - The Investigatory Powers Act in 2016, this Act is known as the 'Snoopers Charter' and can be described as a highly intrusive state-sanctioned surveillance power that does not require judicial authorisation. This Act further permits a huge number of agencies within the British intelligence community to have access to the data and information gathered, as well as carrying out the surveillance power themselves. Even after the 2013 Snowden revelations, that led the NSA and the United States government to amend their laws and introduce

---

more safeguards and oversight mechanisms, the United Kingdom adversely responded by introducing a Bill that simply placed previous surveillance conducts by the government on paper to make them official, thus, to completely infringe on personal privacy. Hence, Britain can be said to carry out blanket surveillance against its own people.

As it is with American surveillance, a complicated relationship exists between national security and privacy due to the continuous threats of terrorism and espionage that drive governments to act in certain ways that eventually lead to privacy infringements. Nevertheless, unlike the amended legislation dictating the conduct of surveillance in the United States, existing UK law - the Investigatory Powers Act of 2016 - is incomparable to any surveillance or intelligence legislation in the West due to its disregard of individual privacy. Although this Act was passed by parliament, it raises issues of legitimacy due to the unlimited access that authorities have, which may eventually be misused. In quoting Liberty, a Human Rights Organization, arguing that the Act, "makes us all less safe, and less free."[179] In addition, from a future perspective, Britain should expect that due to the Investigatory Powers Bill, it may

---

[179] Thomas Beamont, The Round Up- Snoopers Charter set to become law, One Crown Office Row (Dec 1, 2016), https://ukhumanrightsblog.com/2016/12/01/the-round-up-snoopers-charter-set-to-become-law/

face increased human rights scrutiny by both tech corporations and human rights groups.

Ultimately, besides the upcoming Brexit and its implications, what makes the future of Britain alarming is the willingness of the current conservative government to abolish the Human Rights Act and replace it with a British bill of rights.[180] In quoting Elizabeth Denham, the UK Information Commissioner, "I don't think Brexit should mean Brexit when it comes to standards of data protection."[181] Thus, Denham's position reflects the leaving the EU should not mean leaving behind negotiated European regulation, including those related to data protection. Nevertheless, securing a victory for human rights - specifically the right to privacy - in British law is central to any Brexit settlement under the May administration. Although the United Kingdom may be on its way out of the EU, the aforementioned cases and EU laws nevertheless significantly affect the United Kingdom as it is still a member of the EU and must therefore comply with EU law and the ruling of the CJEU. Finally, as the Human Rights Act 1998 stems from

---

[180] Jon Stone, Plans to replace Human Rights Act with British Bill of Rights will go ahead, Justice Secretary confirms, Independent (Aug 22, 2016), http://www.independent.co.uk/news/uk/politics/scrap-human-rights-act-british-bill-of-rights-theresa-may-justice-secretary-liz-truss-a7204256.html
[181] Commissioner, UK 'must avoid data protection Brexit', BBC: News (Sep 29, 2016), http://www.bbc.com/news/technology-37512419

higher law, hence the EU Charter of Fundamental Rights and Article 8 of the ECHR,[182] unlike the Investigatory Powers Act of 2016, should influence the 2016 Bill and nothing else ought to be conventional.

4. Recommendations

Following the 2013 Snowden leaks on both American and British government surveillance programs, a conflict arose between the intelligence community and the public. Moreover, the United States' foreign relationships with various states became strained, for instance, with Germany and Brazil.[183] Similarly, the United Kingdom faced consequences, such as facing distrust by the public as polls conducted in 2015 reflected that most of the participants favoured Snowden's actions of disclosing such programs.[184] Thus, how are both governments going to fix such disparity between the intelligence community and individuals? This now falls upon the administrations in both nations. Could President Trump and

---

[182] Article 8 of the European Convention on Human Rights. "Everyone has the right to respect for his private and family life, his home and his correspondence."

[183] Snowden disclosed that the NSA targeted Merkel (Germany) and Rousseff (Brazil)

[184] Jonathan Cable, Working Paper - An overview of public opinion polls since the Edward Snowden revelations in June 2013, UK public Opinion Review (June 18, 2015), https://sites.cardiff.ac.uk/dcssproject/files/2015/08/UK-Public-Opinion-Review-180615.pdf

Madame Prime minister May, find middle ground to these surveillance issues and strike a balance between national security and individual privacy in this digital age? This section is to propose how government surveillance programs ought to be in the near future. Hence, this could be a model followed by 'all' nation states. The discussion will recommend undertaking a privacy by design approach when introducing such laws.

In democratic nations, individuals are expected to be protected from the overreaching scope and nature of governmental surveillance operations to avoid having their privacy infringed upon. Regardless of the phrase being attributed to system engineering or even the internet, here we seek to relate the phrase 'privacy by design' to the process of promoting privacy from the outset when designing laws related to conducting surveillance. This could further be related to having the laws themselves impose a requirement upon data holders or co-operative nation states to protect the information or data from being misused or disclosed to unauthorized personnel when being transferred from one end to the other.

Taking the aforementioned into consideration, and with the expected re-authorization date of section 702 approaching by the end of this year, the United States Congress should thoroughly reform the law in order to restore the privacy rights of Americans as well as others. Such measures should include a total prohibition on the backdoor searches loophole that permits the government to access information or data relating to American persons, and impose restrictions and clear cut regulations when data is shared among the agencies and ensure that there is proper oversight when it comes to each agency. Thus, Congress here would be limiting what agencies can do with the information acquired as the aforementioned loophole is considered as a gap in the privacy protections Americans are constitutionally entitled to. In addition, despite the NSA recently announcing that it will be prohibiting 'about' searches in April 2016, such a prohibition should be explicitly included in the law if the Act is to be re-authorized by Congress. Hence, such efforts to close this loophole should be included in the reform package Congress will be proposing at the end of the year.

In addition, Congress should restrict the government from accessing privileged information or communications under section 702, such as that between an attorney and client, or a doctor and patient. Congress should further limit the expansive definition of 'foreign intelligence information' as the current definition does not solely relate to terrorism, but also permits agencies to search the information for multiple purposes including investigating ordinary offences. Ultimately, Congress should place another sunset deadline to provide thrust and open the door for possible reforms in the future.

In relation to Great Britain, the government should reconsider the entire 2016 surveillance Bill as it largely infringes upon privacy. The Investigatory Powers Act of 2016 is still a question of trust for the public, and could probably be perceived as a privacy disaster. As has been mentioned in the second chapter, the GCHQ's interception of the fibre optic cables to acquire private communications through its Tempora program results in a significant number of data and information being staggered. Hence, this type of surveillance affects the privacy of probably every single person who uses the internet in the United Kingdom.

Even though the Investigatory Powers Act of 2016 have just been recently enacted, we propose that it is to be repealed and replaced by a new comprehensive surveillance law that is more protective of privacy rights. Also, instead of the indiscriminate bulk collection provided in the current Bill, there must be a restriction in that all interceptions of communications or fibre-optic cables be targeted to a specific person or group. Most importantly, and following the United States approach - under section 215 of the USA PATRIOT Act and section 702 of FISA - the Bill should only authorize the collection of metadata, not the content of communications.

Another point that Britain, should take into account throughout its Brexit negotiations, is the fact that the Investigatory Powers Act is in conflict with the upcoming General Data Protection Regulation (GDPR), which is to be enforced across all EU member States in May 2018. One might wonder whether the GDPR might be enacted in Britain seeing as Britain is projected to leave the EU soon. This is very likely to occur as the projected date of Brexit will be 2019. Nevertheless, the issues of the GDPR's application to Britain may still be unclear.

The Investigatory Powers Act and existing as well as prospected EU law may be in conflict, and the UK should consider prioritizing the GDPR and current EU directives over its own arbitrary enacted laws, or else it will face scrutiny from both the privacy community and fellow EU Member States. Ultimately, the Investigatory Powers Bill can be considered inadequate in protecting persons from intrusions into their private information and it is a clear example of unnecessary and grossly disproportionate surveillance.

General Remarks & Conclusion

Privacy today faces threats from a growing surveillance norm justified in the name of national security. With the increased number of terrorist attacks occurring globally, it is undisputed that intelligence is vital in combating terrorism and espionage. Nevertheless, privacy safeguards and protections are necessary in ensuring that a legitimate process is followed in the collection of foreign intelligence as well as ensuring that there exists an appropriate balance between the privacy of persons and national security.

Lawmakers in the United States are of the opinion that the USA Freedom Act introduces considerable amendments to American surveillance under section 215 of the USA PATRIOT Act, despite barely touching the surface of section 702 of the Foreign Intelligence Surveillance Act. On the other hand, British lawmakers should consider adopting more adequate safeguards such as those in the United States. This includes minimization and targeting procedures, transparency requirements, and congressional oversight. The Privacy and

Civil Liberties Office in the United States certainly had an integral role in introducing new laws and amending existing ones to help preserve and protect the privacy of individuals. A similar approach by Britain would be welcomed by the public and privacy proponents.

Ultimately, America has made considerable strides in strengthening privacy safeguards for its individuals, while also enabling the government to obtain the necessary communication records that are essential to investigations involving terrorism or espionage. Britain's position is still unclear as to whether we will see changes in its current surveillance law, yet the GDPR may force Britain to introduce or even enhance the privacy safeguards of its individuals due to the conflict it will have with certain provisions of the anticipated GDPR.

* 9 7 8 1 9 7 9 2 7 0 3 5 9 *